LOVE COLUMNS AND READER FAVORITES
FROM POST-DISPATCH COLUMNIST

BILL McCLELLAN

Credits

Illustrator • Dan Martin

Designer • Wade Wilson

Copy editor • Frank Reust

Sales & Marketing • Lisa Clark & Jessica Pryor

Special thanks to Doug Weaver of Kansas City Star Books

Softcover
ISBN 978-0-9842084-9-4

Printed by Walsworth Publishing Co., Marceline, Mo.

To order additional copies:
Call **1-877-767-8785** or go to **www.thepost-dispatchstore.com**

Dedication

To Mary, who was told by a fortune teller that she would meet an unkempt young man with long hair. She then moved in next door to me, and realized, that like it or not, the whole thing was fated to be.

Contents

Introduction

Originally, I was going to write a standard foreword. I would start by explaining how the book came to be. I wanted to do a collection of love stories. The bosses wanted it to be more expansive, so we agreed I would pick out half the columns – they could be (and are) love stories – and readers would pick out half the columns.

Less work for me. Cool.

Then Dan Martin showed me the cover he designed. I realized I didn't have to write a foreword. I could just plug in another column. Even less work for me. So let me just say thanks for picking up this book and I hope you are lucky in love.

MAY 25, 1995

My hero! Hey, wait a minute: I think I know that guy

Some friends from New Orleans sent me a book the other day. It was a paperback, published by Silhouette Desire. It was titled "Immoral Support." The art on the cover was that of a man and woman embracing. The woman was lost, as they say in this kind of book, in the throes of passion. The Gateway Arch was in the background.

My friends had not put a note in the package. Naturally, I was puzzled. Why would they send me a romance book? I'm a true-crime kind of guy.

I opened the book, and read the author's acknowledgments.

"Dedicated to the unsung heroes of the St. Louis press, none of whom made it into the pages of this book but were an inspiration just the same."

So I started to read the book. The chief male character was a ruggedly handsome newspaper reporter. In the words of the author, he had a smile worthy of a toothpaste ad.

Here is more of the author's description of the reporter: "His features were strong, his eyes a light blue-gray that reminded her of a stormy ocean. His dark brown hair was quite unruly and long enough to cover the collar of his leather bomber jacket."

Hmmm, I thought. I don't own a leather bomber jacket, but the rest of the description, particularly the part about the unruly brown hair, sounded very familiar.

Eventually, I came to the plot. The handsome reporter was writing a true-crime book. The crime involved a man from another city who came to St. Louis for a convention. The man's wife died an untimely death in a hotel bathroom. The state claimed the man had murdered her. The man claimed he had been out jogging.

I read that and did a double-take. Then I flashed myself a smile worthy of a toothpaste ad.

This book was about me!

I am, as regular readers know, the author of a true-crime book. The book was about the Ed Post case. Post was a businessman from New Orleans who came to St. Louis for a convention. His wife died in the bathtub of their hotel room. The state claimed Post had murdered her. He claimed he had been out jogging.

No wonder the people from New Orleans, whom I had met, not incidentally, during my research into the Post case, had sent me this romance book.

I was thrilled, and I say this despite the fact that while I am, as the romance author suggested in her acknowledgments, an unsung hero, I am not entirely unsung.

In fact, I have been mentioned in three books. Mystery writer John Lutz once had a character reading one of my newspaper columns right before an airplane exploded. In Harper Barnes' novel "Blue Monday, " a police reporter bore my name. Finally, I was quoted in "Under the Influence, " the unauthorized biography of the Busch beer dynasty. That book was written by Peter Hernon and Terry Ganey.

But in each of those three instances, I was a very minor character. In "Immoral Support, " I am the guy.

Mel Riggs is the name I go by in this book. I am a ruggedly handsome and extremely resourceful reporter. Without putting too fine a point on it, I should add that this is a romance book, and when I say that I am depicted as being wondrously talented in certain aspects of my personal life, I trust that adult readers will know what I'm talking about.

While the author has certainly nailed me, I should add that, for comic relief, she has added a newspaper columnist to the mix. He's a slob, known more for his gaudy ties than his sexual prowess.

Except for his job as a columnist, he could have been modeled after a number of my colleagues here at the newspaper.

Although I enjoyed the book very much — and what guy wouldn't enjoy reading a romance book in which he is cast as the hero? — I am not advising aficionados of the Post case to rush out and buy "Immoral Support."

There is very little about the case itself in this book. None of the cops are even mentioned. The prosecutor is mentioned only briefly. He is described as a guy who looks like a walrus.

This is, I'd say, a little bit of poetic license. Dean Hoag, the real prosecutor in the Post case, does not look like a walrus. Not exactly like a walrus, anyway.

Besides, this book only takes the Post case up to the point where things get fouled up because the sheriff's deputies were hosting parties for the sequestered jurors. There is nothing about the second trial, and nothing about the second appeal, which seems like it's going to lead to a third trial.

In truth, the book is fun but predictable. I get the girl, the Earth moves a few times and so on.

Now, if you'll excuse me, I think I'll go out and buy a leather bomber jacket.

DECEMBER 29, 2013

A St. Louis love story that's still being written

In the summer of 1941, a dashing young newspaperman took his girlfriend to the Admiral on the riverfront, and said, "Mae, I'd like to take you out on New Year's Eve," and then he paused, "of 1999." How romantic, she thought.

They had met in the summer of 1935. Martin Duggan was an Irish kid who lived in a German neighborhood on the south side of St. Louis. Mae Mosher was a German kid who lived in an Irish neighborhood on the city's north side.

Mae went to St. Joseph Academy where she was best friends with Martin's sister, Geraldine. (Geraldine would later become a Sister of St. Joseph of Carondelet.) Martin went to South Side Catholic High School.

One day in the summer of 1935, Mae came to visit Geraldine. Martin was eager to meet his sister's best friend. He was working that summer as a soda jerk at the Penguin, an ice cream parlor just down the street from his house on Connecticut Street. On his breaks, he carried ice cream to Geraldine and Mae. How thoughtful, Mae thought.

The following summer, he took her to the Muny Opera to see "The Great Waltz." It took him two or three streetcars to get from his house to hers. They eventually caught the Muny Opera Special at Lindell and Vandeventer. He bought $1 tickets, which, in those days were right behind the boxes. How extravagant, thought Mae.

Truth be told, it was a bit of a one-sided relationship in those days. Mae was smart, attractive and popular. Martin was smart.

In fact, he was smart enough to earn a scholarship to St. Mary's University in

San Antonio. He went to Texas in September 1938. Mae went to Harris Teachers College here in St. Louis.

After his first year in college, Martin got a summer job at the Globe-Democrat. He was a copy editor in the Sunday features section. He earned $20 a week. More importantly, he was morphing into a dashing newspaperman.

He ran into Mae that summer at an event at the Kiel Opera House. Montana Sen. Burton K. Wheeler, an isolationist and an America Firster, warned against getting drawn into the war that was already looming over Europe. It was at this rally that Martin and Mae reconnected. Mae said, "You should come over and see my mother's new wallpaper." How strange, thought Martin.

But he was over the next night. It should be noted that Mae's mother cared more about bargains than color combinations. The ceiling was yellow and blue plaid. The curtains featured pictures of Davy Crockett. The window shades featured Hopalong Cassidy. The new wallpaper was red and black with pictures of Chinese junks.

Martin appreciated women who valued bargains. He and Mae became a couple. They exchanged letters when Martin went back to Texas, and they dated the following summers.

On a Sunday morning in December 1941, a friend burst into Martin's dormitory room. "The Japanese bombed Pearl!" he shouted. Like most Americans, Martin had never heard of Pearl Harbor, and he thought the Japanese had bombed the Pearl brewery. That seemed like a strange thing to do, but Martin was, after all, from a brewery town, and he instinctively knew that this meant war.

He worked at the Globe during that Christmas break, and Managing Editor Lon Burrowes – an idiosyncratic fellow who had dropped the "e" from his last name – asked Martin if he'd stay on full time. Martin was making $25 a week during the break. He started to explain to Burrowes that he was too close to graduating to quit, but Burrowes interrupted him. "Could you get married on $45 a week?" he asked. "Mr. Burrowes, I could do anything on $45 a week," Martin responded. He made arrangements with St. Louis University to finish the class work he needed for a degree.

On Valentine's Day 1942, Martin proposed. The proposal came in Mae's living room with the red and black Chinese junks on the wall and the yellow and blue plaid ceiling. Davy and Hopalong watched as Mae said yes. She and Martin were married on May 26, 1942.

They had five children, four sons and a daughter. (They now have 10 grandchildren and seven great-grandchildren.) Martin became chief of the copy desk and eventually the editor of the editorial page. Mae became the Mother Jones of the school choice movement. They supported each other's efforts.

On New Year's Eve 1999, Charlie Brennan of KMOX was emcee at Powell Hall for a performance of "Die Fledermaus." Brennan offered Martin a role. After the opera was over, Mae joined Martin as the cast danced on stage. He reminded her, of course, about his long-ago comment. How romantic, she thought once again. They expect to celebrate this New Year's Eve at St. Agnes Home in Kirkwood, where they now live.

FEBRUARY 14, 2001

WWII hero took his time and found girl of his dreams

Joe Baruzzini joined the Navy shortly after the Japanese attacked Pearl Harbor. He was sent to flight school, and he became a pilot.

Eventually, he ended up on an aircraft carrier in the Pacific. He flew air support for the Marines at Okinawa, and he earned the Navy Cross – the nation's second-highest medal – for his part in sinking a Japanese cruiser in the final days of the war. He also received a Distinguished Flying Cross for his role in sinking a battleship.

One morning, he received orders to bomb an electronics factory in Tokyo, and he was flying toward that city when orders came to abort the mission and return to the carrier. The war was over.

His aircraft carrier, the Ticonderoga, was among the ships in Tokyo Bay for the Japanese surrender.

Baruzzini came back to the states with plenty of money. After all, there had not been much opportunity to buy anything while floating around on an aircraft carrier in the Pacific. Before returning to civilian life, he wanted to take advantage of the big discounts at the PX or Ship's Store, as it was called in the Navy. But what should he buy?

A lot of the fellows were buying rings. Engagement rings, wedding rings. These were young men getting ready to start their lives. Baruzzini was 24 years old, a war hero. He looks handsome in the old photographs. He didn't have a girlfriend, but he figured that would soon change. He bought an engagement ring and a wedding ring.

He came home to St. Louis. (OK, the answer is Soldan High School.) He used the

GI Bill to go to Washington University. He graduated with a degree in mechanical engineering. He was a co-founder of Ross & Baruzzini Inc., an engineering-architectural firm that is still going strong. In his spare time, he flew hang gliders.

So he was successful in all ways but one. He didn't meet the girl. He put the rings in a safe deposit box in the bank. He retired in 1986 at 65.

A couple of years after he had retired, a neighbor couple took him square dancing. You need to get out, they said. There, he met Frances.

She was a country girl, raised in Rhineland, and she was pretty and strong of character. She had four children, all grown by this time. When she and her husband got divorced, she went to college. She got her undergraduate degree when she was in her mid-50s, and then she continued on and got her master's. She was working in a hospital when she went square dancing and met Baruzzini.

He noticed her right away. There was much to like about her, he thought, and the better he got to know her, the more he found to like. He took up square dancing.

Eventually, he decided he had met the girl.

Still, he wasn't silly or anything. When you wait until you're past 70 to get married, there is no need to act like a high school kid.

"I didn't propose to her on bended knee," he told me.

Indeed, he didn't. Instead, he drove her to the bank. He opened his safety deposit box. He showed her the rings that he had bought so many years earlier.

"Do you want them?" he asked.

She said she did.

They were married at the courthouse on Valentine's Day of 1992. A simple ceremony, a small wedding. He was 71. She was 67.

They're celebrating their ninth anniversary today. They haven't been square dancing in a while. Baruzzini had a knee replacement in October.

But they seem to be doing just fine without dancing. I noticed, for instance, that Frances, 76, was wearing both rings on the day I stopped by. Nice rings they are, too. I mentioned that, and Frances smiled. So did her decorated Navy pilot, now 80, who bought those rings so many years ago and then waited to meet just the right girl.

JULY 19, 1996

Love can survive divorce, perhaps, even marriage

If you're one of those people who feel bad about Prince Charles and Princess Di, I've got some good news.

Maybe the divorce can get their romance started again. That's what has happened with Mike and Karen Mulikey of St. Louis.

Regular readers might remember Mike. I wrote about him once when he was standing in the hall in the Municipal Courts building. He was waiting for a young woman named Judy.

She was a prostitute. In a curious twist on the old story about a prostitute with a heart of gold, Mike was the cop with a heart of gold. He had first seen Judy in the holdover. She was eight months pregnant.

"You remember something like that," he told me.

Later, he saw her on the street. Somebody had beaten her up. Mike asked her about her baby. She said the state had taken it away. Apparently, it had been born addicted to cocaine.

Mike decided to help her. He brought her home.

"It was the day before my birthday," Karen recalled earlier this week. "Not that it was a surprise or anything. He'd told me about her. I agreed that we'd let her live with us and help her out."

It didn't work.

Judy would run away, and then she'd come back, and finally she stole Mike's service revolver. He reported the theft, and then Judy came back and tearfully told

Mike that she had traded his gun for some cocaine at a crack house. Mike reported that news to the detectives working on the theft, and when they went to the crack house, the proprietor explained that the fellow who had ended up with the gun had gone to Kansas City but was expected back in a few days.

Mike's superiors were not happy.

"A drug-addicted prostitute who's living with you traded your gun for crack, but we're going to get it back as soon as the crackheads are finished with it?"

That's what happened. The cops ran ballistic tests to determine if the gun had been used in any open shootings here or in Kansas City while it had been out of Mike's possession. It had not.

Still, Mike was suspended for 10 days for associating with a known felon.

More than a year later, Judy showed up again, and this time she was sick. Mike, who by this time had retired from the department, agreed to take her to the hospital, and when he went upstairs to talk to Karen, Judy was gone. So was some money. So was his gun.

She was arrested the following day, and it was for these thefts that she was due at the courthouse on the day I met Mike. She didn't show.

I asked Mike if he felt at all foolish.

"I don't regret anything," he said. "In the end, you have to answer to The Man upstairs."

What a fine fellow.

I then lost track of him until I ran into Karen a couple of weeks ago. I asked how Mike was doing.

"We got divorced," she said.

"Oh, I'm sorry," I said, but I wasn't shocked. Some people are too good. Maybe Mike was one of those. Maybe Karen got tired of him trying to help people who don't want to be helped.

Turns out that wasn't the case.

Instead, Karen had quit drinking. Truth is, she used to drink too much. I'm not being down on her. Princess Di used to make herself throw up. Prince Charles ran around with an old girlfriend. Everybody has a bad habit or two.

Including Mike. He, too, used to drink too much. That's important to understand. When you have two people drinking too much and one quits, you've got a problem.

So they decided to get divorced. That was late last year.

They filed for divorce, and things began rolling along. This was the second marriage for each, and they had only been married for five years, so there wasn't much of a fight about who gets what. Each would keep his or her own things.

Then Mike quit drinking.

Soon they were seeing each other again, but the divorce continued to roll through the system.

"We thought about stopping it, but we already had the court date, and we decided to just let it happen," said Karen. "I mean, we could always get married again."

By the time they went to court for the divorce in April, they were living together again. They walked out of the courtroom holding hands.

They're still together. You might say they're happily unmarried.

"It's strange," Karen told me. "We were happy before we were married, and we're happy now that we're not married. We were only unhappy when we were married."

You see, there's hope for Charles and Di.

FEBRUARY 25, 1998

Woman learns you really can't sell your love

"The money's just for the room, babe. The love is free."

So go the words to the old song, but isn't there always a cost to love? Is sex ever free? You wouldn't expect such heavy philosophical questions to be debated in St. Louis County Court, but those were the very issues that formed the heart of the lawsuit heard Monday afternoon in the courtroom of Associate Circuit Judge Sandra Farragut-Hemphill.

S.E. Freund was suing Ellie Bush for $2,500.

Freund is 78 years old. He is an investment broker, a member of our city's elite. His name occasionally appears in Jerry Berger's column when my colleague mentions the names of those well-heeled and kind-hearted souls who support various charitable endeavors. Lest our S.E. Freund be confused with some other S.E. Freund, the adjective "deep-pocketed" sometimes precedes Freund's name.

Bush is 63 years old. You could throw a lot of adjectives in front of her name – attractive, spirited and well-preserved all come to mind – but deep-pocketed does not. She sells commercial real estate, but not often.

In July 1991, Freund loaned Bush $2,500. He went to a stationery store and bought a standard promissory note. He filled in the blanks. For interest rate, he put zero. There was no repayment schedule. It was an open-ended, no interest loan.

Bush signed it.

Five and a half years later, Freund demanded his money.

By that time, however, Bush had talked to people about this loan. She contended that the main consideration for this loan had been the granting of sexual favors.

According to her, she and Freund had been dating, but their relationship had not crossed over to the physical side until after the loan. She had needed money, she told people, and there had been an unspoken but implied understanding about the loan. She had, she said, lived up to her part of the bargain.

If that's the case, said these people, then the promissory note is invalid. It is illegal to exchange money for sex, and any contract that would seek to validate such an illegality would itself be invalid.

The real question was this — Would a respectable woman be willing to go into a courtroom and testify under oath that she had willingly accepted money for sex?

I don't have $2,500, said Bush.

And so the battle was joined.

You can imagine how eagerly I awaited the trial. So many important questions were open to debate. Is love ever free? Are relationships ever equal? Is there such a thing as a lonely old rich guy?

No, no and no is what I'd say, but I vowed to keep an open mind.

Bush and Freund sat across the table from each other, and I gave the early pretrial edge to Bush. She seemed more comfortable, more resolute.

This puzzled me. Hers was the greater humiliation. Where was the shame in what he had done? To be able to pay for sex, and to want to pay for it at his age, well, I know fellows who'd sign that contract.

Meanwhile, the lawyers argued their respective positions to the judge.

Frank Susman, who represented Freund, maintained that Bush should not be allowed to use her sex-for-money defense. That's not in the contract, he insisted.

"She was part and parcel of any such implied deal. She can't raise the argument now," he said.

Sadly, the judge agreed with Susman, and so nothing of philosophical bent was presented at the trial. In fact, the only witness was Freund. He testified that he loaned Bush the money, and he identified the promissory note, and that was that.

Oh, there was the slightest hint of intrigue when Freund admitted under cross-examination that he also sent $1,000 to Bush — after the $2,500 and this time without a promissory note — but for unknown reasons, she returned the money within days.

Barred from discussing the philosophical underpinnings of her case, Bush did not testify. And so she lost.

As did the rest of us who had been hoping for a deep and meaningful discussion about relationships.

FEBRUARY 14, 2010

Ex-salesman takes a shot, closes the deal

Bill Melnick was born in Brooklyn 87 years ago. He enlisted in the Army Air Forces in the early days of World War II. He was 20 years old and had never been more than a few miles outside of the New York City area.

He was sent to the West Coast and then Scott Field — now Scott Air Force Base — for training as a high-speed radio operator in Morse code. He met Edna Feldman at a USO dance. They were married four months later. Then Bill was sent to a small weather base on Southampton Island in the Canadian Arctic Archipelago, where he spent the duration of the war.

After the war, the couple settled in St. Louis. They had two daughters and a son. Bill was a traveling salesman. He sold women's apparel in Missouri, Illinois, Kansas and Nebraska.

In the postwar days, there were hundreds of small independent clothing stores in Bill's territory. Sometimes a store owner wouldn't want to look at whatever line Bill was selling. Bill would point to his car parked outside. "You see that car? It's completely paid for, and all from commissions from this very line. That's how popular this line is."

Traveling the same roads, but with different lines of women's apparel, was Fred Seigel. He was from University City. He also enlisted in the Army in the early days of the war, and he met a girl at a USO dance in St. Louis. Fred had come in from Fort Leonard Wood. The girl's name was Mitzi Journman. Fred asked if he could take her home. No, she said. But he called the next day.

They were married after the war.

Mitzi had grown up in St. Louis, and her dad, Ellis Journman, was an apparel salesman who had become an activist in the National Association of Women and Children's Apparel Salesmen. So that's how Fred got into the business. His territory covered Missouri, Kansas and Illinois.

He and Mitzi had two children, a son and a daughter.

The Seigels and the Melnicks knew each other, and when a fashion season ended, Mitzi and Edna would sometimes swap leftovers from their husband's respective lines. The leftovers could be had, of course, at great discounts.

One of the Melnicks' daughters went to Sunday school with the Seigels' son, and the Melnicks' son was friends with the Seigels' daughter, but the two couples never really socialized. They were friends, but not close friends.

Fred died seven years ago. He and Mitzi had been married for 56 years. Edna died two years ago. She and Bill had been married for 64 years.

Last spring, Bill's kids, concerned that he had become a hermit since their mother's death, urged him to get out of the house. Go to some senior activities at the temple, they said. He was a member of United Hebrew Temple.

So he went to the seniors' event in May. He walked in and saw Mitzi sitting at a table with a mutual friend, Tiby Stone, whose husband, Sid, is a retired women's apparel salesman.

Bill walked over to the table and said to Mitzi, "Would you go out with me?" Mitzi, who had not dated since Fred's death, stunned Tiby by saying, "Sure." Bill leaned over and whispered, "I've gone out with other people, but nobody as pretty as you." Mitzi turned to say something, but he was gone.

The activity for that meeting was a speaker, and he was something of a windbag, but who cared? Bill had asked Mitzi out, and she had said yes. It would be difficult to say which was more surprising.

Bill left without getting Mitzi's phone number, but he called the Stones, and got the number from Tiby.

They went out for burgers. They have been going out ever since. In November, they went to Atlanta to visit one of Bill's daughters. She wrote Mitzi a note: "Dad is very lucky to have such a warm and caring lady. Come back soon."

All of the kids on both sides have been like that, Mitzi told me when I visited last week. All of the kids are happy that they're happy.

They continue to maintain their own homes, and they are not thinking about marriage, but they are very much a couple. I asked Bill if he was nervous asking a woman out for the first time after more than 65 years. Or maybe a salesman can't let the fear of rejection stop him, I suggested. He smiled, and I thought of the young man who used to point to his car. "You see that car? It's completely paid for ..."

I asked what they would be doing on Valentine's Day. "I have a special thing for her that she doesn't know about," he said.

"You do?" she asked.

By the way, I take a special interest in the couple because I was the speaker on the day they got together.

JANUARY 14, 1985

What's rat poison among friends?

Burt Reynolds starred in a movie called "The Man Who Loved Women." I didn't see the film, but I read a review written by one of my colleagues. Apparently, Reynolds played a sculptor who fell in love with every woman he met and remained in love with his old loves even as he was falling in love with new ones.

What a stale plot! What a waste of an excellent title! Here in St. Louis, we have a man whose story, if it were told on the silver screen, would deserve the title.

His love is so strong that he requested I not put his name in the newspaper.

"I don't want to bring no trouble down on anybody," he said.

I don't like to use pseudonyms. But in this instance, I will. I'll call our hero Burt.

Burt lives on the city's near north side. The house he lives in is a bit raggedy, as is Burt himself. He's almost 60, and on Friday morning, when I visited him, he was unshaven. He was also surprised that I had heard of him. I explained that some cops I know had spoken of him. How did his name come up, he wondered. I said that the cops had been talking about unusual crimes. One of the cases that came up in the conversation was the Shirley Allen case.

Burt grinned.

Shirley Allen is the woman who allegedly spiked her husband's beer with antifreeze. She was supposed to have done it on a regular basis. Her husband eventually died, and Mrs. Allen was convicted of murder.

Oh, I remember that one, said Burt.

That's not surprising. One of Burt's wives — he's had several — tried a similar thing with Burt. She put rat poison in his coffee. She allegedly did it on a regular basis for about six months. Burt knew something was wrong. He felt sick all the time. His stomach felt as if it were on fire.

"I thought I had an ulcer," he said. "I tried everything. For a while, I drank goat's milk. The only thing that made me feel better was whiskey."

Finally, a relative caught Burt's wife in the act, and she confessed. At last, Burt knew what was wrong. He spent more than a month in City Hospital, where the doctors repaired, as best they could, the damage to his stomach and intestines.

Well, people are always doing horrible things to each other. Rat poison in the coffee would be worth a few stories on cold nights, when the cops are dawdling over reports, trying to gain a few extra minutes of warmth. But Burt's case entered the legendary status when he decided not to prosecute.

"Didn't want to get her in trouble," he said. "Didn't then. Don't now."

She was, Burt explained, 20 years younger than he. And it wasn't hate that led her to the rat poison, it was love.

"She was a jealous little thing," Burt said. "And I'm afraid I gave her reason to be. I drank a lot and ran around. Besides, what good would it do to send her to the peniteniary? I just wanted to get away from her."

Burt is remarried, but he has remained friends with the woman who fed him rat poison. In fact, he has remained friends with her family. Her family, incidentally, was angry with her when they learned what she had been putting in Burt's coffee. Still, Burt and his new wife occasionally get together with his ex-wife and her family.

"Sometimes I'll mention rat posion to her, and she'll just laugh," Burt says of his ex-wife. "I laugh, too, but I'm careful around her. One time we were over at her sister's for dinner, and I wouldn't eat anything because she had helped prepare the food. I wasn't trying to be nasty or anything. I just wouldn't have been able to enjoy the food, knowing that she had been in the kitchen."

While Burt and I were talking, his new wife asked if we wanted coffee. I declined the offer, but Burt accepted.

"She treats me real good," he said of his new wife. "Takes care of me like I was a baby."

She smiled and went into the kitchen. A few minutes later, she put a cup of coffee in front of him.

"You don't feel you should watch her make it, huh?" I asked kiddingly.

Burt laughed and said he wasn't worried. Besides, he added, he used to drink it with cream and sugar, so the color was milky, anyway, and the cream probably disguised some of the taste of the rat poison.

"I drink it black now," he said.

We talked for a few more minutes. I assured Burt I wouldn't use his name or his address.

"It's not me I'm concerned about," he said. "I don't want anybody thinking I'm trying to dredge up a case against my ex-wife. Like I told you, I don't want to get her in trouble."

As I left, I glanced at his cup. The man who loved women had finished his coffee.

MAY 28, 2007

Flowers express devotion to pilot killed in WWII

In the spring of 1944, as Frannie Dolan was finishing her junior year in high school, she met Francis Xavier Kelly. He was in training at Scott Air Force Base with one of Frannie's neighbors, so she got fixed up with him. They went to the Powhatten Theater in Maplewood and then to the Priscella Shop for a soda. They did this several times during the summer before he was sent overseas. They exchanged letters through the fall, winter and into the spring.

Then Kelly's parents called. His plane had gone down over Germany. After the war, the bodies of the crew members were brought to Jefferson Barracks National Cemetery for a mass burial. Frannie attended the service.

Decades passed.

Two years ago, Fran Noonan, the former Frannie Dolan, was at Jefferson Barracks National Cemetery for a Memorial Day service. She decided to visit Kelly's grave site. She found fresh flowers and a note. "My dear love Bart, I miss you very much. Love you with all my heart forever." Fran was puzzled. She looked at the names on the common stone: Frances F. Golubski, Aram G. Kadehjian, Francis Kelly Jr., Horace B. Lane, Joseph H. Mull Jr., Irving Smarinsky.

Last year, Fran visited the grave site again. There were more flowers and another note. "Bart sweetheart. I think of you so much and I love you forever. Your devoted Marian."

Fran went to the florist. He took her name and number and said he'd give them to the woman who had sent the flowers. Later that day, Marian Love called.

Marian grew up in a small town in Iowa. When she finished her junior year of high school in the spring of 1944, she went to California to spend the summer with her brother and his wife. Her brother was in the Army Air Forces and stationed at March Field near Riverside. Marian got a job on the base as a typist. After work, she would swim at the officers' pool.

That is where she met Horace Bartlett Lane. He was 21 years old. He had grown up in Seattle. He had started college at Washington State University. He was majoring in chemical engineering, but dropped out to enlist. He wanted to be a pilot. He saw Marian in the pool and offered to give her swimming lessons. He was very polite, very serious.

Several days later, he asked her to dinner. They began seeing each other every day. He was waiting for an assignment to a B-24. He would then be headed to the war in Europe. In late August, he was assigned to a crew. He would be leaving in a matter of weeks.

Marian and Bart had been telling each other that they were engaged to be engaged, but now with his departure imminent, Bart gave her a ring. But when to get married? After the war? Marian wrote her parents. I want to get married now, she said. Her parents initially balked, but then agreed. How could you pretend things were normal in the midst of the war?

They were married on Sept. 8 in a small church on base and then went to Los Angeles for a two-day honeymoon. A few nights before he left, he was stretched out on the bed. He told Marian that he had been offered a training position but had turned it down because he wanted to stay with his crew and do his part. Now he regretted the decision. He looked terribly sad.

On Oct. 6, he left. Marian returned to Iowa and went back to high school.

She wrote her husband every day. Long letters, always upbeat, never mentioning the fear that ate at her.

In early March, his letters stopped. On March 20, she received a telegram. He was missing.

On March 3, the formation of B-24 bombers crossed the English Channel and was about 40 miles north of its target of Madgeburg, Germany, when the Messerschmidts attacked. One of the bombers was hit and fell into the B-24 that Bart was co-piloting. A gunner and bombardier managed to bail out. They were later captured and eventually released. The others went down with the plane. Among them was the radio operator, Francis Xavier Kelly.

Of the 19 members of the two planes, three survived. The others were buried in a common grave in Madgeburg.

Marian graduated from high school and moved to Seattle to be with Bart's parents while they awaited his return. The war ended, and there was no word of Bart. Marian enrolled at the University of Washington. In March 1946, a year after he had been reported missing, Bart was declared dead. Marian was a widow. She had just turned 19.

Her father suggested she get a new start. She enrolled at the University of Colorado. At a Halloween dance, she met a tall, serious-looking young man. His name was Bill Love. He was working on his master's degree in engineering. He had been in the Navy during the war, assigned to submarines. His training had ended just as the war had.

Marian and Bill were married in August 1947.

They spent some time in California and then they went to the University of Illinois, where Bill received a Ph.D. in mechanical engineering in 1952. By then, they had three daughters.

Also by then, Bart's remains were at Jefferson Barracks National Cemetery. The remains had been recovered from the common grave at Madgeburg, and eventually, all but six had been individually identified. The remains of those six were reinterred in 1949 at Jefferson Barracks in a common grave.

While the Loves lived in Illinois, they visited the grave site.

Marian was honest with Bill. She had periodic bouts of almost inconsolable grief. He would comfort her during these periods.

In 1970, Bill got a job as a professor at the University of Washington. By that time, Bart's father had died, but his mother was still living, and Marian and Bill would visit. Bill always hugged her. She said she loved him.

Marian always thought the two men were alike. Tall, smart, kind and serious. Both had an aptitude for engineering. Even their names — Lane and Love.

In 1992, Marian and Bill took a trip to England to see the airfield where Bart had been stationed.

Still, it would be wrong to think that Marian was living in the past. She loved Bill. She loved their family. She just didn't want Bart to be forgotten.

Bill always said he understood. Marian let him read the letters Bart had sent her. This is the sort of man I'd want a daughter to marry, Bill said. By the way, the children - two sons followed the three daughters - always knew about Bart.

Bill died in January. Marian had him cremated. When she dies, she will be cremated and their ashes will be buried together.

In the meantime, she sends flowers to Bart.

MAY 1, 1998

This couple marks a whole new chapter in the book of love

As I listened to the Father of the Bride chastise his new son-in-law in the courtroom Thursday morning, I thought, "This marriage is not going to last."

Which means that it probably will. As far as this case is concerned, I have guessed wrong at every turn.

The case had its official beginnings in April of 1997 when Robert Murray of Hazelwood shot his pregnant girlfriend, Andrea Caldwell, in the head. The fetus died, and Andrea was not expected to live. Murray contended the shooting was an accident, but the state was supposed to have some information indicating that the relationship had been a rocky one.

So Murray was charged with murder in connection with the death of the fetus and first-degree assault in connection with Andrea's injuries. As soon as Andrea died, the assault charge was going to be kicked up to murder.

But Andrea didn't die. She came out of her coma and verified Murray's story. The shooting had been accidental.

Geez, I thought. This is a wonderful story. The victim turns out to be the star witness for the defense.

You see, the charges were still hanging out there. The murder was eventually knocked down to involuntary manslaughter, and the assault was knocked down to second degree, but the state still wanted something.

"Even if it was accidental, it was still reckless conduct," prosecutor Doug Sidel told me. "It's like driving when you're drunk."

A good analogy. Murray was basically going with the Dumb Guy defense. He had been drinking and had not known the gun was loaded.

I went out to talk to Andrea. She was again living in Murray's house.

As a reporter, you're supposed to be a blank slate and not try to guess what somebody is going to tell you, but I'm not always good at that, and I figured that Andrea was going to tell me that he was showing her the gun when it suddenly went off, and that losing the baby was the worst thing that ever happened to him, and they had been planning on getting married and so on.

Wrong.

She said she didn't remember the night of the shooting. (A bullet to the head can do things to your memory.) She shook her head when I asked if they had been planning on marriage — Bobby didn't seem ready to settle down, she said — and, no, Bobby wasn't exactly thrilled about the baby.

"I think he was coming around to it, though," she said.

Uh, fine. But if you don't remember the night of the shooting, how can you be so sure it was accidental?

"Bobby told me."

There was, it turns out, evidence of a sort to back up that claim. Shortly after the shooting, the magazine for the automatic handgun was found hidden in the bathroom. When she came out of the coma, she told the authorities that she had hidden the magazine some weeks earlier. She didn't want a loaded gun around the house. Kids might come over.

Apparently, neither she nor Murray realized a round could be in the chamber even if the magazine were absent. That's consistent with the Dumb Guy defense.

Our interview was terminated, incidentally, by Murray's mother, who said she had come over to help make Andrea comfortable while she talked to a reporter.

Well, I may have been wrong about what Andrea was going to say, but one thing I felt I knew for sure. This relationship was not going to last.

Murray would stay with her only until the legal rigmarole was finished. As soon as he didn't need her testimony, the relationship would be history.

The case was presented to Judge Robert Lee Campbell earlier this month. He found Murray not guilty of manslaughter, but guilty of assault.

Sentencing was Thursday morning, and Campbell was lenient. He suspended imposition of sentence, and placed Murray on five years' probation. If he successfully completes his probation, he won't have a record.

As is often the case in criminal court, the proceedings had the feeling of a wedding. That is, the defendant's family sits on one side of the courtroom and the victim's family on the other.

In this case, though, the victim sat not with her family, but with the family of the defendant. By the way, she's not just a victim. She's a bride.

She and Murray were married on Valentine's Day.

So I was wrong again.

When the judge asked for victim's impact statements, Andrea's father used his time to berate his new son-in-law. He talked about the nightmare that Andrea's family has been through, and then he mentioned the wedding.

"Our nightmare continues," he told Murray. "You have made us your in-laws."

There are, I'm sure, a good many Fathers of the Bride who have felt that way, but few have had the opportunity to say so in open court.

Then Andrea made her statement, and said how much she loved Bobby. She also announced that she was pregnant.

In the hall afterward, I noticed Andrea hugging her mother, and then she walked away with Murray and his family.

I wouldn't bet on the marriage, I started to tell a friend, but then I stopped myself. In this case, I have constantly been surprised.

APRIL 4, 1986

Wedding ceremony was a labor of love

Susie Mayberry and Rory Parker were Popeye sweethearts. They fell in love three years ago while working together at Popeye's Famous Fried Chicken & Biscuits store on North Kingshighway.

Like so many young people — Susie is now 23, Rory is 25 — they decided to live together before they got married. They planned a big church wedding.

It was scheduled for the end of April. Events intervened, and the decision was made to move the date up. Everybody agreed that the marriage ceremony should beat the baby.

I should emphasize that Susie was not unhappy about being pregnant. She was thrilled. She wanted to start a family. She definitely wanted to be married first, but aside from that, it didn't matter when the baby came.

The date of the wedding was moved up to last Sunday. As per the original plan, the ceremony was scheduled to be held at the Pentecostal Saints Tabernacle on this city's North Side. The Rev. James Stewart, Susie's uncle, was going to preside. Susie and he figured on a crowd of about 300.

The wedding was scheduled for 3 p.m.

Susie woke up Sunday feeling strange. Rory took her to the Lutheran Medical Center, where they had taken their Lamaze classes to help them through the labor process. Susie went into labor.

Rory called Rev. Stewart and asked him to perform the ceremony in the labor room. He agreed, and said he'd be over as he soon as he drove a van-load of passengers home. Picking up, and taking home, parishioners is a service the church provides.

The van broke down at Kingshighway and Oakland.

Rev. Stewart called the Earl Greene Towing Service. Greene runs that business out of his home. He also does minor road repairs. He'll change a tire. He'll jump-start a car.

Sunday is often a pretty good day, probably the best day of the week for dead batteries. People who don't get out much during the week will want to go to church, and discover that their car won't start.

Greene had towed Rev. Stewart's van before. Several times. So the two men are friends, and when the minister explained the situation, Greene didn't even think about the dead batteries he'd miss. He agreed to take Rev. Stewart to the hospital. They hooked the van to the the tow truck, and off they went.

I don't know if you've ever been in a delivery room during labor, but it's hectic. The nurse and the doctor — when he's there — are busy checking monitors and dials. They don't have time to do much else.

Besides, it's kind of tacky to have a delivery-room nurse be the witness at a wedding. Better to have a relative or friend, but since none had arrived by the time Rev. Stewart reached the hospital, why not the tow-truck driver who had been nice enough to tow the van to the hospital?

Greene had not been present at the birth of his own children. He remembers pacing nervously in the waiting room, the way men handled the birth of their children in the days before Lamaze.

But if a witness is needed a witness is needed. Greene went into the delivery room to witness the marriage.

Susie said "I do" between contractions.

So Susie Mayberry became Susie Parker, and two hours later, Sherrell Dominique Parker entered the world. She weighed 6 pounds, 2 ounces. An alert, healthy child. The first person to hold her was her father, her mother's husband.

I visited Mrs. Parker in the hospital a couple of days later.

She was in a happy mood, as befits a new bride or a new mother, let alone a young woman who is both. She laughed about the circumstances of the ceremony, but said it really did mean a lot to her to get married before the baby came.

"I'm a religious person," she said, and then she laughed again.

"The Lord says, 'No shacking,' " she said. "Have mercy on me."

Mrs. Parker said that with a smile, as though she were confident that the Lord is indeed merciful. Clearly, Mrs. Parker's Lord has a sense of humor, too, as well as a sense of timing.

As for the other participants, they all agreed that it was a charming, if unusual, ceremony.

“I planned a longer service for my niece,” said Rev. Stewart. “But if I’m in a cramped situation, I can shorten it up. That’s what I did.”

Greene downplayed his part in the whole thing.

“Let’s just say it wasn’t an ordinary day for me,” he said. “Truthfully, I was just happy to help.”

MAY 6, 2007

What's two weeks in the county jail to a fellow who is lucky in love?

Friday morning was wet and dreary, and the St. Charles County jail is hardly a cheery place even on a sunny day, but Greg Roeder looked positively beatific as he sat on a bench in the third-floor waiting room. My first thought was that he was one of those perverse types who enjoy watching somebody else having a bad time. I was the somebody else.

I was at the jail to see David White. He is facing two counts of possession of a controlled substance. He is a persistent and prior offender, so he is facing some serious time. He was supposed to have had a preliminary hearing Friday morning, but when I checked the docket posted outside the courtroom, I didn't see his name. A woman from the prosecutor's office checked with the judge. "He'll have to be rescheduled," she said. "The judge has recused himself." I asked why. She shrugged.

When I realized White wouldn't be in court, I went over to the jail. Maybe I'd be able to see him. I took the elevator to the third-floor waiting room. I asked the deputy if I could see White. I'm not on his visiting list, I said.

Are you a lawyer?

No, a newspaper reporter.

The deputy left to consult with a higher authority. He came back in a couple of minutes. You need permission from Capt. Myers, he said. "Fine. Can I speak with the captain?" He's not in today, said the deputy. "Does anybody fill in for the captain when he's not here?" The deputy said something to the effect that he didn't think it would do any good, but he'd ask. He left.

I looked around. There was one other person in the waiting room. He seemed to be smiling.

The deputy came back. He said the captain would be back on Monday. I could try again then. The deputy left the waiting room, and I headed to the elevator. The smiling man spoke. Crazy place, he said, or something to that effect.

"Are you waiting to see somebody?" I asked.

Oh no, he said. I owe them two weeks, and I've taken some time off work. I'm going to spend my vacation here.

He told me he was 37 years old. He said he was getting his life in order, and after he gave the county these two weeks, he would be free and clear. Most importantly, he was back with his first wife, the woman he has always loved.

As regular readers know, I have a soft spot for love stories. I pulled out my notebook and sat down.

He said that he and Bonnie had gone to high school together, but she had not been attracted to him. "She thought I was a dork." When they were both 21, they met again, at the Dirty Duck bar in St. Peters. They were married in May 1994. They had two children, but then the marriage went bad. It was all his fault, Roeder said. Drinking, running around, that sort of stuff.

After the divorce, Roeder continued on his downward spiral. He fell behind in child support payments. The state suspended his drivers license. "I didn't even know," he said.

He and Bonnie both remarried and then divorced. Perhaps when there is one person in the world for you, that is to be expected.

One night he was pulled over and then arrested for driving on a suspended license. It was that sort of minor trouble, he said, that led to him owing the county a couple of weeks.

But none of that mattered because he and his wife had gotten back together. He said that his own folks had gotten divorced and then remarried. That is exactly what he has in mind, he said. He added that he'd love to get remarried on his anniversary, but he was still going to be in jail. Nevertheless, this trip to jail was redemptive in nature, a second beginning.

Suddenly, the deputy reappeared. He explained that I did not have permission to talk with Roeder, who was, more or less, already in custody. But he wasn't yet locked up, I argued. Doesn't matter, said the deputy.

No problem, I said. I left feeling pretty good. Roeder's good spirits had lifted my own. Besides, it's an ungrateful man who complains about getting kicked out of jail.

NOVEMBER 15, 1985

Hoping for luck with the Irish

Had you been listening to Radio Telefix out of Dublin, Ireland, last Tuesday morning, you would have heard talk-show host Gaye Burne urge the women in the audience to listen closely.

Pay this some attention, he said. That prosperous American bachelor you've been hearing about, the one who's coming to Ireland to find a wife, he's going to be our next guest. Joseph Carter lives in a 10-room house with a swimming pool in the back yard. He's on the telephone now from Saint Looie, Missouri, in the United States. Carter, who is a caretaker at a condominium complex in West County, got on the phone. Yes, Gaye, I'll soon be there, he said. I'm looking forward to my visit.

Carter flew to Ireland on Wednesday. He will be there for three weeks. It could be the trip of a lifetime.

Last month, in preparation for his visit, Carter placed an ad in nine of the largest papers in Ireland. He specified that the ad should be in bold-face type, and that a box should be placed around it to set it off.

The ad said that a college-educated, attractive, prosperous American bachelor would soon be visiting Ireland to find a potential spouse. Attractive and intelligent women up to the age of 32 (Carter is 40) were invited to respond in care of the newspaper. Carter would pick up the responses when he arrived.

With each ad was a letter to the appropriate editor.

"You might find my request and method of finding a spouse a bit unusual. I agree with you," Carter wrote. "Nonetheless, if you feel this search is worth a small feature article or back-page filler, be my guest."

It was the kind of letter, and the kind of story, that editors love.

To help any editor who wanted a story, Carter included a resume. He listed his occupation as "property manager and estate management." He mentioned his interests in horticulture and writing. He remarked that he had been published "in a minor way."

Well, Carter does manage some property. He has to cut the grass, so that would qualify as an interest in horticulture. The boss complains if the horticulture gets too long. Carter indeed has been published. His letter to the editor about Memorial Day was eloquent.

He said he lives in a 10-room house with a swimming pool in the back yard.

The converted carriage house in which he lives does have 10 rooms, although Carter uses only two of them. The condo complex does have a swimming pool, although technically it belongs to the condo owners rather than the help.

But he low-keyed his financial status.

"Our American ladies want to know about this first. I don't tell them," he wrote. "It has nothing to do with who and what I am."

In the weeks before his trip, two reporters from Irish newspapers called him to get further information. Carter had not seen their stories before he left, but he seemed confident that the stories were of a positive nature. After all, the radio station got in touch with him.

Carter, by the way, is a true son of Ireland. His great-grandparents came from the old country.

And Carter is very serious about finding an Irish wife. If he meets Miss O'Right during his three-week visit, he intends to tell her the truth about his occupation and his 10-room house.

Besides, if the truth were known, Carter's not doing too badly. He's got a steady job, and he doesn't have to pay rent, so he can save some money. He has a nice truck. He also has a fine personality, and a lively sense of humor. I'm not good at judging another man's looks, but he's certainly not bad looking.

In fact, he probably could have told the truth in his ad, and he'd still have sounded like a good catch. But with women, sometimes it's best to get them interested before you hit them with the facts.

Carter knows that. For the last couple of years, he's been active in the growing movement to meet people through the media. That is, he places ads in the personal sections of the Riverfront Times and St. Louis Singles. He responds to ads in those publications. He has been on the KMOX radio date line. He has made almost 200 contacts.

But none has worked out.

Some of the women haven't had the decency to respond to his responses. Others have, but didn't suit his tastes. Several did suit his tastes, but he didn't suit theirs.

One of that last batch seemed to like him at first.

"Then I told her I was a caretaker."

So maybe it makes some sense to lead a lass on for a bit. Give her a chance to know you, and like you, before you hit her with the truth.

That's Carter's theory. We'll see how it worked, and what kind of response was awaiting him in Ireland, when he comes home.

JUNE 9, 1999

Walking couple left their mark before vanishing

Mary Louise Hawkins spent her career in education, so it goes without saying that she met some interesting people. There were so-so students who went farther in life than any of their teachers would have imagined, and there were go-go students who unexpectedly slowed down. There were colleagues and bosses and parents. Lately, though, her thoughts have turned more and more toward two people she never met. She saw them on a daily basis when she worked at McCluer North High School and then the nearby Ferguson-Florissant School District Administration Building.

She figures she must have seen them for 10 or 15 years. They used to walk up and down Waterford Drive.

"They walked that same stretch at an agonizingly slow pace," Hawkins writes. "She was a physically challenged person, short in stature, with one leg unable to bear its share of weight. This leg was dragged behind with a foot twisted at a peculiar angle. Step, drag, Step, drag. To passers-by, it looked like this crab-like way of walking caused her deep agony. She faced toward the outside of the sidewalk, the street side, with a hard grasp on her companion's arm. His sustaining arm was bent at the elbow and clutched to his stomach as though it took very little effort on his part to assist her. His mincing steps that looked so ungainly allowed him to walk at a pace she could sustain.

"He was very tall. So tall that he had to stoop just the slightest bit so she could reach his arm and still keep her balance. He bent toward her as though he were listening intently to something she was saying. But in all those years, no one ever saw them speak to each other as they traversed this bit of sidewalk in Florissant. Those of us who worked in either the high school fronting their route, or in the central offices of the school district located next door, saw the couple daily. Rain or bitter cold did not deter them. Intense heat of summer seemed not to faze them either. If one were to travel on Waterford Street in the morning to attend a meeting to be held across town, they would be walking. If one returned to school in the late afternoon, they would be walking again. One could not help but wonder if they were walking still, rather than again. They never seemed to smile. They were never seen to laugh.

"Most of us working in those locations took note of them, but we never discussed them with each other. The couple just never came up as a subject of our conversations. But we all knew them. Then, at some point this past fall, they stopped walking. After more than 10 years of daily walking that stretch of sidewalk at such a torturous pace, they just never were seen there again.

"Had her unknown illnesses finally taken her away, freeing him from his daily chores. Or maybe plunging him into a deep abyss of sadness, a loss of purpose? Had they moved together to some new place, to learn by micro bits another sidewalk with a new group of passers-by to notice not to notice?"

Mary Louise Hawkins retired without knowing.

She stays in touch with her former colleagues, and none of them know much, either. Some say the couple had been walking for 15 years, others say 10. Everybody seems to agree that the tall man and his short companion were last seen in the fall of 1998.

One of Hawkins' colleagues, a walker herself, says she used to pass them on her walks and exchange greetings. The woman had a deep voice, the man a soft one.

Knowing of my fondness for old love stories, Hawkins wrote me. Perhaps somebody who reads the paper will see your story and know something, she said.

When a retired English teacher – and couldn't you tell by her writing – makes a request that could lead to an old love story, how could I turn her down?

JUNE 11, 1999

Couple that was Florissant fixture thrives in Florida

They met at the Casa Loma Ballroom in the fall of 1954. Marie was 20 years old, and lived in North St. Louis. She took care of her father and two brothers. Bud was an electrical maintenance worker who lived on the city's South Side.

One night the manager of the ballroom asked Bud if he had a dancing partner. Bud said he didn't. The manager looked around and saw Marie. He introduced the two. They never stopped dancing.

There was no need to actually date. They'd just meet at the Casa Loma three or four times a week. Mostly, they were ballroom dancers, but they were quite the jitterbuggers, too. In fact, they did jitterbug exhibitions on the Admiral. They weren't paid for these exhibitions. They just did them.

A couple of months after they met, they began to formally date. Of course, it was dancing dates, and generally at the Casa Loma. Instead of meeting at the Casa Loma, Bud would go to Marie's father's house and pick her up and later take her home. It was as if they formalized something that had been understood.

They were married in July 1955. They spent a couple of days at Pere Marquette for their honeymoon. Then it was on to life.

In those early days of marriage, they lived with Marie's father in his home on Montgomery Street. The dutiful daughter needed to watch her dad. He died in 1960, and Marie and Bud moved to Florissant. By this time, they had two children.

Bud worked as a dispatcher for a trucking firm.

On April 19, 1976, Marie had a bad headache. She didn't think anything about it.

Maybe it had to do with stress. Bud's mother had died three days earlier. In fact, Marie first noticed the headache at the funeral home.

It turned out to be an aneurysm that had burst in her brain. Marie was in a coma for three weeks. When she woke up, she was paralyzed on her left side. That would be a permanent condition, the doctors said.

The doctors also said she should try to walk.

So she did. They did, actually. There was no way Marie could walk alone. She had no balance.

They walked up and down the sidewalks in the Thunderbird Hills subdivision. But despite the name, there weren't much in the way of hills and so they soon changed their route for more of a challenge. Up and down Waterford Drive they began to walk.

They did so for years.

Their hours varied depending on Bud's shift. When he worked the night shift, they walked in the afternoons. When he worked the day shift, they walked in the mornings.

They became a part of the landscape. And then one day, they vanished.

A retired English teacher, Mary Louise Hawkins, wrote me a letter. She said she had seen the couple every day, in all kinds of weather, when she worked at McCluer North High School.

She said the walking couple had touched so many people's lives. Their story seemed to be one of devotion and love. But what had happened to them?

I printed Hawkins' letter. I then got a call from Debbie Kastcrup. The people you wrote about are my parents, she said. Their names are Bud and Marie Frederich, and they have retired to Florida.

I called them. I told them that a number of people had called to say that they, too, remembered the walking couple. You two were famous, I told them. I asked if they had known that.

"People used to honk. We didn't pay much attention," said Bud.

I said that people were inspired by them.

"My husband is an angel," said Marie. "I once had a doctor tell me that a lot of women would take my disability if my husband came with it. I told the doctor I'd keep them both."

They now live in Lakeland, Fla., and yes, they spend much of their time walking. In their new place, they have a picture of the Casa Loma Ballroom, a reminder of the time when they were dancers, before they were walkers.

JANUARY 16, 2013

New lease on life with rekindled love

Can a man love two women? Can a loving, faithful husband have a special place in a corner of his heart for an old girlfriend?

Consider the life and loves of Joe Brader.

He was born in July 1925 in a two-family flat on Milentz Avenue in south St. Louis. His mother was the housekeeper for the priest at Sts. Peter and Paul Catholic Church in Soulard. His father sold cemetery plots for the Sts. Peter and Paul Cemetery on Gravois Road.

When the cemetery was filled in 1928, the church opened a new Sts. Peter and Paul Cemetery – now Resurrection Cemetery – on MacKenzie Road.

The church used the first floor of a farmhouse on the site as an office. The Braders lived on the second floor. Two of Brader's three siblings were born in the cemetery.

Brader was a sickly child. He had been born with a tumor on his chest. He was not considered healthy enough for surgery until he was 3. At 5, he developed an infection in his ear that also required surgery. According to family lore, doctors predicted he would not survive.

His father eventually got out of the cemetery plot business and opened a bowling alley – Bowling Grand. The family moved to Webster Groves. Brader dropped out of school when he was 15 to work with his dad.

He turned 18 in 1943 and was drafted. He completed training in time to be shipped to England in May 1944. He was in England for all of 12 days before climbing aboard a landing craft for D-Day. He landed on Utah Beach.

Actually, near Utah Beach. The landing craft opened its doors too early – perhaps because of the shelling — and Brader stepped off the craft and went under water. He struggled to the surface and started to swim. His pack weighed him down. He had a life preserver, but he couldn't get it to work.

He seemed to be getting nowhere. He looked up and said, "Lord, I'm done."

He realized he was lying on the edge of the beach. He saw the bottom half of a man's body next to him. He got up and ran over the beach and onto a road.

He was a medic for the combat engineers. His unit helped build a bridge over the Rhine. His mother died while he was in Germany. He learned of her death in a letter from a cousin. He stayed in Germany until January 1946. Then he came home and was mustered out.

He went back to work at the bowling alley.

One day a young woman came in and wanted to rent left-handed bowling shoes. That meant rubber soles on the left shoe, leather on the right. (It has to do with sliding a foot.) There were none in her size, so she ended up borrowing Brader's shoes. That's how he met Ann. They dated a while and then drifted apart.

He married another girl he met at the bowling alley. He became a tile installer. He and his wife, Betty, had two sons. They had a long and happy marriage. Betty died suddenly in October 1999. After 49 years of marriage, Brader was alone. He was bereft.

Four months later, he called Ann.

I have a friend, very happily married, who still loves an old girlfriend. He will always love her. I admire him for that. His old love has no bearing on his present love. I think of Simon and Garfunkel. "She once was a true love of mine." Once and always.

Had Brader, in some corner of his heart, always loved Ann?

"I wouldn't say I thought of her a lot," he said.

But he began thinking about her on a Thursday. He thought about her all day Friday. Saturday morning, he picked up the phone book and looked up her maiden name. There were a couple of listings. He called one.

The woman who answered was Ann's sister-in-law. She said Ann still lived in the area. Was she married? She was a widow. Brader asked Ann's sister-in-law to give Ann his number. Tell her we met at the bowling alley, he said.

She called that day. It was the first time they'd spoken in 54 years.

Like Brader, Ann Westhouse had had a long and happy marriage. She had five children. All grown, of course. She invited Brader to her house. It was a big house. "This ain't going to work out," thought Brader.

But 13 years later, it seems to be working out just fine. In fact, on the calendar in Brader's kitchen, Feb. 26 is circled. That's the date he reached out to Ann.

One thing seems certain. A new love — or an old love rekindled — is good for a person's health. Brader, the sickly child, seems robust. Last Saturday, he received an award from the Red Cross for donating blood. He has donated 200 times. He didn't start until he retired.

He swims, plays golf and, of course, bowls. He said his most recent scores were 205, 203 and 211.

FEBRUARY 3, 2010

Investigator has his eye out for cheaters

Brian Randant and I walked into a bar in St. Charles early one evening last week. Several young women were at one end of the bar. They were laughing and talking with one another. Maybe they worked together and were enjoying a happy hour before going home.

At the other end of the bar were a group of guys. They were in blue-collar work clothes. They seemed to know the bartender well. Regulars at the bar, I'd guess.

Randant and I gave the two groups a brief glance and then moved to a table.

"There they are," he said, but he didn't point. "The couple playing pool."

There were several pool tables across the room. I stole a quick look at the couple, and when I realized they were lost in their own world, I allowed myself a longer look.

She was blond, pretty and small. I knew she was 40, but she looked younger. Her billiards partner was thin and had long, dark hair. He was younger than the woman by a few years.

Randant already had shown me her photo. It was a heart-breaking picture. She was smiling in front of a Christmas tree. The heart-breaking thing was that her husband had given the photo to Randant, a private investigator. His company is called "Catch Em' Cheatin.'" If you hire him, he will follow your spouse around. If he finds evidence, he will take videos indicating that your spouse is cheating.

I say "indicating" because he does not try to sneak up to windows and take videos of people inside apartments or motel rooms. Instead, he'll take videos of people coming out of apartments or motels. Or videos of people hugging or sneaking a quick kiss in a parking lot.

He wasn't taking pictures in the bar. He was just giving me an idea of the business.

After the husband hired him – at $75 an hour for a minimum of four hours – Randant had plotted his strategy. This was supposed to be the woman's night out with the girls. So Randant had two of his employees follow her. They followed her to the bar. There was a guy waiting for her.

Randant and I were at a restaurant near the woman's home. The employee called to tell us where she was. We drove to the bar.

We chatted at the table while they played pool. I asked what would happen next. He said that when the couple left, his employees would follow them. If they went to an apartment or motel, they'd get videos of them when they left the apartment or motel. That's considered pretty good proof in this business.

I asked Randant if his business was hurt at all by the recession. Just the opposite, he said. When the economy goes bad, his business gets better. He has a theory about that. He figures that relationships get frayed when people have money problems. Or maybe when reality gets bad, people try to escape it.

Actually, he has theories about a lot of things related to cheating. He thinks a lot of guys cheat for the excitement of cheating. He thinks most women are less likely to cheat on a whim. For them, it's a more serious thing.

It gets complicated, he said. And seamy. He said he'd rather own a restaurant. But he added that his job is not to figure out why people cheat, only to catch them doing it.

He said that Fridays and Mondays are big nights for cheating. That's because most people use work as an excuse for staying out late. If the weekends are out, Friday becomes emotional because the cheater won't see his or her lover until Monday, and Mondays are big because the cheater hasn't seen his or her lover for two days.

Are there many false alarms in this business? Randant said a man will hire him if he suspects his wife is cheating, and quite often that suspicion will prove unfounded. But by the time a woman hires him, she pretty much knows, he said.

By the way, sometimes a man will be angry that Randant has found no indication that his wife is cheating. Maybe it's because he's cheating, Randant said. Again, it's complicated.

Any cases he won't take? If a guy tells Randant that he's going to beat the hell out of his wife if she's cheating, Randant won't take the case. Also, no police officers. "If either of these two were cops, we wouldn't be here," he said about the couple playing pool.

Shortly thereafter, our quarry and her friend left. Randant and I stayed behind. A few minutes later, he got a phone call. The couple had gone to another bar. "We can't go," he said. "They might recognize us."

The next day, Randant called. After the couple left that second bar, they went to a third bar, and then they went their separate ways. No motel, no apartment.

Well, who knows? There's nothing wrong with playing pool with a friend. That's what I thought — hoped, actually, as I recalled the photograph — until Randant said they had video of them kissing and hugging in the parking lot after they left that third bar.

MARCH 2, 2008

From Cuba, with love: No dictating what heart knows

Maria Flores and Orlando Recio were married 62 years ago in Havana, Cuba. In the wedding photo, Maria looks radiant in her white dress. Orlando is movie-star handsome in his police uniform. He and his bride are walking under a canopy of swords held by fellow officers.

Maria had grown up in Santiago, a city in southwest Cuba. Her father, Pedro, was a self-made man. He had come from a poor farming family. As a young man, he carted produce into the city to sell. He saved his money. He sent his three children to college. Maria became a lawyer. She was about 30 when she met Orlando at a party. She saw him across the room. How could she not? At 6-foot-4, he stood out in a crowd. He spotted her, too, and soon they were talking, laughing. From that first moment, she knew they would marry.

They began dating, but in the traditional way — that is, with a chaperon. Usually, Maria's younger brother filled the role.

Maria and Orlando were married in March 1946. Sixteen months later, they had a daughter, Adelina.

The family moved to Santiago, and Orlando worked for his father-in-law. By this time, Pedro Flores was a successful businessman. For the most part, Maria stayed home and cared for her daughter. In the 1950s, there were rebels in the mountains, but the idea of revolution seemed far away. Maria took a case in which she represented a man who was accused of having ties to the rebel leader, Fidel Castro. Mostly, though, their lives seemed unaffected by politics.

Castro toppled the government in 1959. Pedro Flores was arrested and sentenced to prison on trumped-up charges. Orlando knew somebody in the new government, and Flores was released. Still, it was a chilling event.

In November 1960, Maria and Orlando sent their daughter to live with relatives in Miami. In July 1961, they joined her.

In those days, Cubans were allowed to leave the country, but they were allowed to take only some clothes and one box of cigars. Before granting permission to leave, the government would send someone to the house to take inventory. No one was supposed to take wealth out of the country.

Maria and Orlando arrived in Miami with virtually nothing. They were starting over in their early 40s. They stayed with relatives. Orlando got a job at a hotel. He parked cars. Maria became a baby sitter. While taking English classes, she heard that Indiana State University was sending representatives to Miami to interview Cuban professionals and would be offering scholarships to some of them. Maria interviewed and was offered a scholarship. The family moved to Terre Haute. There was an opening in the program, and Orlando was accepted. They began studying to become teachers.

So Orlando and Maria became high school Spanish teachers. Maria got a job at Webster Groves. The family moved here. Orlando got a job teaching Spanish to Peace Corps volunteers, and then he got a job at Kirkwood High School.

The years went by. They became U.S. citizens, and proud citizens, too. But still, they sometimes talked wistfully of returning to Cuba.

In some ways, they were still the couple in the wedding photo. Orlando was a dashing figure, the sort of man who went to a party and was soon surrounded by people. Maria was quiet. But she ran things, said their daughter, Adelina. "She was the brains of the operation, but she made the decisions in such a way that he thought he was making them with her. They complemented each other so well. She was always blindly in love with him, and he relied on her completely."

When Orlando was in his 60s, his health began to fail. First, it was arthritis; then, a form of Parkinson's.

"It was sad to watch," said Adelina. "This tall guy, always so strong, and his body was failing him. She did everything for him."

Two months ago, Orlando, who got around with the aid of a walker, fell in their home. Maria could not get him up. She called 911. The paramedics told Orlando they were going to take him to the hospital. He refused to go. Maria leaned over and wagged her finger at him. "You will," she said. "All right," he said.

Doctors determined he had fractured two vertebrae in his neck. He was sent to St. Luke Hospital's Surrey Place to rehab.

Shortly before Valentine's Day, Maria fell and broke her hip. She was taken to Missouri Baptist Hospital. She had surgery. She came out of that surgery fine, and the plan was to reunite the couple at Surrey Place.

They were frantic being apart. Adelina was running from one hospital to the other, assuring each that the other was fine. Then on Thursday night, Valentine's Day, Maria seemed to weaken. Adelina left her and went to see Orlando. He seemed fine, but in the early morning hours that Friday, Adelina got a call. Her father had died. Adelina could not bear to tell her mother. In the morning when she visited her mother, Maria asked, "How is he?" "I just saw him," said Adelina casually. In the early morning hours Saturday, Maria died.

She died without knowing Orlando had died. Or did she? A doctor said to Adelina, "He must have put in a spiritual call to her."

Three days later, Fidel Castro announced his resignation.

MARCH 5, 2010

Divorce court story ends with a twist

Allison and Yvette were on the uncontested divorce docket Wednesday, and inquiring minds in the St. Louis County courthouse crowd wondered how Judge Dennis Smith would handle the case. If gay marriage is illegal in Missouri – and it is – how can the state sanction gay divorce?

Divorce court is not a happy place, but as these things go, the uncontested docket is somewhat civilized. These are couples doing their own divorces. They don't have lawyers. In legalese, they're going pro se.

But while these cases lack the rancor of contested divorces, there is something immeasurably sad about the assembly line nature of the process. The court can churn through a dozen in an afternoon.

The Wednesday afternoon docket kicked off when Tiffany Hytruck, an attorney from the court's resource center, spoke to the solemn-looking people assembled in the courtroom. "I am not your lawyer," she said. "I do not represent you." She explained that she was there to look over their paperwork before they went in front of the judge, who would, in effect, pronounce them single.

There were several couples in the courtroom. Some sat close together. Some sat a few icy feet apart. There were also a number of women who had come without husbands. Maybe the men had just said, "The heck with it."

There were two women sitting together across the aisle from me. I figured they were the people I had come to see. I nodded at them. They looked away. I took that as a good sign.

The judge appeared and took his place on the bench.

"I always advise people to get lawyers," he said. He explained that if a mistake were made, that mistake could be corrected, but it would be costly to do so.

A young woman sitting next to her husband coughed softly, and as she did so, she covered her mouth, turned toward her husband and coughed into his shoulder. It was an intimate gesture, rife with tenderness, and I wanted to say, "Get out of here! Don't do this!"

The judge asked, "Who had trouble getting into the courthouse today?" A smattering of hands went up. The escalator at the front entrance is broken, and courthouse visitors are led up a dark staircase. "Wait until you try to leave," the judge said.

Although the remark was meant to lighten the mood, it further darkened mine. The escalator has been broken since Christmas. That seems to be the way of things today. When things break, they stay broken. One of our two elevators at the newspaper has been down for weeks.

The judge briefly explained the procedure. When a couple were called to the bench, the one who had filed the petition for divorce would be on the left. The judge would review the paperwork, ask a few questions, and that would be it. "When you go out that door, you'll be single," he said.

The first couple were called to the bench. The woman was on the left. The second couple were called. The woman was on the left. The third couple were called. The woman was on the left.

The court went into a short recess, and I approached the two women across the aisle. "Allison? Yvette?" They were not them.

I spoke to the bailiff. He told me that, despite what the name suggested, Allison was actually a man. He was not in the courtroom. Yvette had come alone to get her divorce. The judge granted it.

I fled the courthouse. Thursday morning, I visited the judge. I said I had gotten depressed watching all those marriages come to naught.

The judge said the work is not as depressing as it seems. "You have two people, and yes, their relationship has ended, but they have decided to work out their differences fairly. Many of them have gone through mediation. And many of these marriages were very brief."

I asked if he ever tried to talk a couple out of a divorce. Very occasionally, he said. He said that if he senses a hesitation on somebody's part, he'll ask if they're sure about the decision to end the marriage. "Once or twice, a couple has decided to try again," he said.

He has sympathy for the people who come before him. "Every one of these files is a story, a love story gone wrong," he said, as he pointed toward a stack of files on a table.

Sympathy but not empathy. "I've been happily married for 33 years," he said, "so I don't see myself in these cases. But I'm not so good with money, and when I used to do bankruptcy, that was different."

By the way, how would the court handle a request for a divorce from a gay couple who had been married in a state that allowed gay marriage?

Smith smiled and shrugged.

FEBRUARY 24, 2007

Children say father was more wonderful than advertised

Don Bopp was born in 1923, and he grew up in Kirkwood. His upbringing was middle class. He was 19 when the Japanese bombed Pearl Harbor. He and his best friend, Lou Greenwell, joined the Marine Corps together.

They fought in the Pacific. They were together at Tinian, Saipan and Tarawa. Lou came out of the war unscathed. Don was wounded at Tarawa. His wound, by the way, was in the rear end. He made a lot of jokes about that. He had tried to run, but he wasn't as fast as he thought he was. Stuff like that. He didn't need much to make a joke. He went to St. Louis University on the GI Bill. He studied journalism. He also worked as a bartender at the Ten Mile House Tavern in Affton. He graduated in January of 1950, and a couple of weeks before he graduated, he ran an ad in the Post-Dispatch.

"Young man, 26 years old, ex-GI, forced to seek employment because of graduation from college. Bachelor's degree with journalism major; available after Feb. 1 unless G.I. insurance refund check arrives; has studied marriage laws of primitive tribes, adolescence in Samoa, ancient history under ancient professors, geology, psychology and women; took enough courses to get a degree; has had experience as a parking lot attendant, stable hand, soda jerk, caddy, material expediter, office clerk, pro at a miniature golf course, drug clerk, in own business, in the Marines and with women. At present is working nights as a bartender, present employer is satisfied or seems to be, can mix a good martini or whisky sour; is a fair dancer but has a lousy voice, can listen sympathetically to tales of woe; is honest but has never been tempted with a million dollars. Can drive a car or tank, but doesn't own either; willing to buy a car but not a tank; believes in God, nickel beer and the St. Louis Browns. Is against communism, women in the

White House and belted-back suits. Will consider any type of employment, but, of course, would prefer an executive position."

Somebody in the city's personnel office must have liked the ad because somebody tore it out of the newspaper. It ended up in a file cabinet, and 52 years later, when Kathy Sullivan was cleaning the file cabinet in preparation for moving the office to the old federal building, she found the ad. She enjoyed it, and she gave it to me. I wrote about it. I wondered in print what had happened to the job-seeker who could drive a tank or a car, but owned neither.

Pete Greenwell contacted me. He's Lou's brother. I remember that ad, he said. Don Bopp wrote it.

The late Don Bopp, sadly enough.

The clever ad did not lead to a great job. Don got a job driving a fuel oil truck. He lived at home with his mom, and he spent most of his evenings hanging out with his friend, Lou.

Then Lou's older sister, Dorothy, moved back to town from Arkansas. She was newly divorced and had four children, the oldest of whom was 14. Dorothy was five years older than Don. She was also a remarkably independent woman for that time. She worked downtown as a manager of a beauty salon and supported her kids. She and Don fell in love, and they were married in a civil ceremony in February of 1956.

The oldest of Dorothy's children, Terry, still lives in town. She was 18 when her mom married Don. I asked her what she called Don.

"Dad," she said. "Maybe that sounds strange, but I guess you had to know him. He was the kindest person you could ever meet, and he had such a sense of humor. Such a storyteller. He'd tell you a story, and you'd be listening intently, and then he'd start laughing and say, 'Nah, that never happened.'"

The younger kids fell in love with him, too. Ray, who was 12 when Don became his stepfather, remembers that his siblings took to Don at once while Ray tried to resist.

"I was the lone holdout," Ray told me. "Everybody else called him 'Dad,' but I called him 'Pop.' I didn't want to be disloyal to my father. I even tried to dislike him, but that was impossible.

"I found him to be a better person than my father, and that troubled me. He was so generous with his time, and he didn't have a bad thing to say about anybody. You couldn't ask for a better father. He was incredible."

Ray, who now lives in California, also remembers Don as the world's best storyteller.

"He could tell you the same story you'd heard 15 times before, and you'd still laugh!"

Don had seen combat in the Marine Corps, but to his new children, he did not come on like a toughie. Just the opposite.

He was afraid of bugs, he told them. He was especially afraid of spiders. So the kids or Dorothy would catch bugs or spiders and scare him. He claimed to be frightened of lightning and thunder, as well.

He and Dorothy had one child of their own, Libby. She now lives in Alaska. Like her siblings, she remembers her father's sense of humor. She remembers how they'd pull up to another car at a stoplight, and Don would pull a tire gauge from his pocket, and pretend to talk into it. "They think I'm a secret agent," he'd say to the delight of his children.

As he said in his ad, he had a lousy voice, but as the kids recall, it was a strong voice.

"He would sing very loud in church — off key, of course — just to annoy Mom and raise giggles from others sitting around us," Libby said.

One day when Libby was about nine, she and her father were walking to a neighbor's potluck dinner. Don dropped the meatloaf he was carrying. He picked it up, brushed it off and took it to the dinner. Neither he nor Libby ate meatloaf that night, but other people did, and one neighbor asked admiringly what the crunchy stuff in it was. Gravel, said Don, and everybody laughed, but nobody laughed harder than Libby.

Twenty-five years after Don married Dorothy in the civil ceremony, they renewed their vows in a Catholic ceremony, and on their 35th anniversary, they were married again in Hawaii. Don told Pete and Lou that marrying their sister was his favorite thing to do.

In 1993, Dorothy died of cancer. Don died two years later. A broken heart, is what everybody said. Don and his bride, which is what he always called her, are buried at Jefferson Barracks.

I know I haven't mentioned his career. He had one. He ended up as a salesman, and although he never became wealthy, he did fine. He also wrote a book that was never published. But it's an odd thing about this story. When I first read the ad and decided to see what had become of the man who wrote it, it was work I was thinking about. What did he end up doing? What kind of a career did he have?

Then I started to learn about Don Bopp, and I realized that work and career aren't really the mark of a man. Pam, who was five when Don married her mother, sent me an e-mail that concluded: "My dad was the warmest, gentlest, most considerate, most honest and tolerant and understanding and caring person I have ever known and he truly loved all of us children equally and he adored my mother." And I realized, without a doubt, that the man who wrote that ad in 1950 did, indeed, turn out to be a very big success.

FEBRUARY 27, 2000

A farm in Warren County provided one couple with a life of plenty

In the early years of the last century, William and Lizzie Hanke had a farm near Bernheimer in Warren County. It was not a river bottom farm. It was a hill farm. Very little of the land was flat. So it was much harder to work than a river bottom farm, and the soil was not nearly as rich.

William's back gave out when he was only 48, and he sold the farm and moved to the nearby town of Holstein. That was in 1928. Had he waited another year, he would have been trying to sell during the Depression, and that would have been next to impossible. Spared from the rigors of his hill farm, William's health returned. He became a hunter. Squirrels and foxes, mostly, but he gained some renown when he killed two timber wolves in one day. He lived to be 92. Lizzie lived to be 90.

Only one of their six children chose the farm life. That was Cora Marie, their second-born. She was 20 when the family moved into Holstein, and she didn't stay in town long. She married Roy Scharnhorst, a young man with a farm on the Missouri River bottom near Treloar. Her youngest sibling, Bill Hanke, who is now 77 and a successful businessman in Atlanta, remembers one of the family's favorite stories about the wedding.

"Dad told her he wanted to give her a present," he said. "She could have either $100 or a mule he had. She didn't hesitate. She took the mule."

There was – and to some extent, still is – a danger with river bottom farms. The river can rise. For the first six years of their married life, the river took most of their crop. Roy and Cora Marie saved enough to eat, and that was it. They came close to quitting the farm but gave it one more year. The seventh year produced a bumper crop.

Years went by. Cora Marie canned food for the winter. She cooked five meals a day — a big, early breakfast eaten in the kitchen, a lighter breakfast she'd take out to the fields about 9:30, lunch at noon back in the kitchen, a lighter meal, snacks really, that she'd take out into the fields in the late afternoon and, finally, a big supper in the evening.

Their marriage produced no children. They were financially stable but not wealthy. They were solid, dependable people, very much at home with the other citizens, mostly of German descent, who work the small farms and live in the small towns in southern Warren County along the Missouri River.

One day, Roy, who was in his early 50s and seemed strong and healthy, went out to feed the hogs and dropped dead. He had never been sick. After almost 30 years of marriage, Cora Marie was a widow. She was 51 years old. She took a job in the general store in Treloar.

Walter Bierbaum farmed the land next to the farm of Roy and Cora Marie. He was a bachelor. He had been a good friend of Roy's and had known Cora Marie since childhood. Neither Cora Marie nor anybody else had ever called Walter by his name. He was known to everybody as Skinny. He was tall, and very thin.

He was the youngest of the six children of Carl and Louise Bierbaum. Carl had rented land to farm on the Missouri bottoms near Treloar. Of the six children, only one stayed on the farm. That was Skinny.

He was a farmer and a singer. In addition to singing in the choir of the Immanuel United Church of Christ in Holstein, Skinny sang at weddings and funerals. Sometimes when bands would come to town, Skinny would be invited on stage to sing with the band.

Still, he was not the most famous of the Bierbaums. That honor went to his older sister, Thalita. She taught school in Warren County for more than 50 years. She began her career in a one-room schoolhouse. Two of her younger brothers, including Skinny, were among her first students. She never married.

When a decent interval had passed after Roy's death, Skinny began to court Cora Marie. Although neither of them were kids, there was nothing hasty about their courtship. They dated for almost seven years. They were married in August 1966.

The Age of Aquarius was dawning in most of the country. The Beatles were singing "Ob-La-Di, Ob-La-Da," and along the river bottom near Treloar, life went on.

Skinny and Cora Marie went to dances on Saturday night. They went to church on Sunday. They worked on the farm all week. They were fun-loving without being adventurous. They seldom left Warren County. They were not the type of people to take a honeymoon, for instance. In 1979, Cora Marie's brother, Bill, came from Atlanta and put everybody in a van and drove them to Florida. It was the first, and last, time that Skinny and Cora Marie saw an ocean.

They had all they needed in Treloar, and the Treloar bottoms. The couple celebrated their 33rd anniversary last summer, but Cora Marie was already slipping. Her failing health concerned Skinny's friends. All his siblings were gone.

Cora Marie went to the Cedar Crest Nursing Center in Washington, Mo. Before long, Skinny followed.

He died Feb. 17. She died Feb. 18. A joint service was held Feb. 19 at the Immanuel United Church of Christ. They were buried in the church cemetery.

The obituaries mentioned that he was a lifelong farmer and that she was a homemaker.

NOVEMBER 25, 2007

A kindness brings woman thoughts of a better time

Janice was born in an apartment above Ollermann's Market on Lackland Road in Overland in 1936. She was the second of eight children of Raymond and Lucille Moore.

Raymond worked at the downtown post office. Lucille had been a seamstress with her own shop on Forsyth Boulevard in Clayton, but she stayed home after the children came. When Janice was just a toddler, the family moved to a house on Hood Avenue. Lucille, who had an eighth grade education, designed the house.

Raymond was drafted during World War II. By then, he had four children, and Lucille was pregnant again. It didn't matter. He went off to training. Several months later, he came home. "The children were never told what happened except it was some kind of medical thing," Janice told me. Her mother, who had been born in the country, announced that the family would move to the country and farm. That did not work out, and they moved back to Overland.

Janice's older brother had a friend, Kenneth Weier. He was five years older than Janice. "He was not interested in me, but I took an interest in him," she said. Eventually, he noticed her. One day when she was 13, Kenneth was outside working on his car. Janice went out to watch him. It was a winter day. Snow was on the ground. Kenneth and Janice began horsing around. He put snow on his glove and washed her face. Janice's brother came outside and yelled at Kenneth. "Get your hands off my sister," he said. "If she doesn't like it, she can say something herself," said Kenneth. Janice didn't say anything. Soon, Kenneth was coming over to see her.

When she was 14 and he was 19, they decided to get married. Raymond and Lucille were strongly opposed to the marriage. Finally, they told Janice, we will talk to the priest and we will abide by his decision. Janice was not happy. "He'll tell me to wait until I'm 40," she said.

Kenneth and Janice and Raymond and Lucille went to the priest at All Souls Catholic Church. The priest listened and then made his pronouncement. "It's obvious that they are in love. If they will wait six months, I will marry them."

The wedding was set for February 1952. By that time, Janice would be 15. Raymond and Lucille said they would not oppose the wedding, but would not pay for it. Kenneth sold his car to finance the wedding. The very first expense was an engagement ring. They went to Zales jewelers in downtown St. Louis. They picked out an engagement ring with three small diamonds.

A few months after they were married, one of the diamonds fell out and was lost. Janice thought she would replace it when they saved some money. "Someday," she thought.

Kenneth had not finished high school, either. He had a factory job. They lived in an apartment in Wellston. Janice got a job in a 5-and-10 store. They both walked to work. Then Kenneth was drafted and went into the Army. The first of their four daughters was born while they were in Germany. Kenneth got out of the Army and went back to work.

Pretty soon, it was clear that "someday" was going to be a long way off. After about 15 years, Janice went to Famous-Barr and had an imitation diamond put in the hole. Still, she never gave up the thought of replacing the fake stone with a real diamond.

Earlier this month, on a whim, she called Zales jewelers in the Chesterfield Mall. She asked to speak to the manager and told him that a diamond had fallen out of her ring 56 years ago. The manager's name is Gary Thomas. He told Janice that the loss was not covered by a warranty. I know that, she said. I am asking for a kindness.

He told her to bring the ring into the store and he would look at it. She did. The jewelry store normally offers a lifetime warranty on stones in rings, but the warranty is contingent upon inspections every six months. But Thomas decided to waive the conditions. He agreed to replace the diamond at no cost.

Janice contacted me. "This is a wonderful Christmas story to warm everyone's heart," she wrote.

I drove to her home in Overland on Friday. I asked her what Kenneth thought of the jeweler's kindness. "I don't know," she said. We split up, she added. The marriage had long been rocky, she explained.

But she was still nostalgic about the ring? "It is a reminder of a better time," she said.

When I returned to the office, I called Thomas. "Yes, of course, I remember her," he said. "She had tears in her eyes." I asked if he knew that she and her husband were separated. "Yes, she just up and volunteered that," he said.

The ring will be ready this week.

MARCH 30, 2012

No need for beagleze in division over dog

Splitsville is an unhappy place, and that's true even for couples who were never married.

Such a couple arrived at the St. Louis County courthouse on Tuesday. They never married, but they have found themselves in Splitsville. They came to court to let a jury decide what they were unable to decide themselves.

Who gets Tilly?

Tilly is a German shepherd-beagle mix. Which side is which? Court records don't say. One sort of assumes that her dad was the bigger dog, but maybe her mother was a German shepherd who liked short guys.

At any rate, our young couple decided at the last minute to waive a jury trial and let Judge Ellen Ribaudo hear the case and make a ruling. She has scheduled a bench trial for next month.

Because she will be hearing the case, she declined to discuss it with me.

According to the court file, the man currently has custody of the dog. The woman has visitation rights. She gets the dog from 10 a.m. Saturday until 8 p.m. Sunday.

The court file does not indicate how the transfer is made, but I was told that one of the lawyers is involved.

The woman's main argument seems to be that she is the one who signed the adoption papers.

That argument does not persuade me. Whenever there is a paper to be signed at our house, my wife signs it. It makes sense to let a woman run things. Now we're going to hold that against a guy?

Then again, I like women who like dogs.

So I'm glad I'm not the judge. This will be a tough case to decide.

Should Tilly be allowed to make the call? In other words, maybe everybody should go to the park and then let the man and the woman each call Tilly and see which one she goes to?

But then you get into dog psychology. Tilly might not go to her "rightful owner." For instance, my dogs would almost surely go to my wife, even though they are more my dogs than hers. But they would be thrilled that she was calling them. Sometimes a dog yearns for the love that seems out of reach.

By the way, I have a dog that is very much like Tilly. When my daughter was teaching at Richmond High School in California, she "rescued" a dog that was hanging around the school. The kids called him "Pop Tart" because that is what they fed him.

My daughter named him Richmond. When she could not keep him in an apartment, she asked if we could take him. If he gets along with the pugs, he's welcome, I said.

So Richie joined us about a year ago. We think he's part beagle, and part pit bull or German shepherd. He thinks he's a pug.

Incidentally, he does not think he was "rescued." He says he was "captured." He sometimes talks about the good old days when he ate Pop Tarts and ran free.

He does not tell these stories to me. I get them secondhand. Mostly from Caesar, one of the pugs. Lucy is more egotistical and talks mostly about herself.

The dogs do not talk to my wife at all, and she scarcely talks to them. Occasionally, she will tell them not to do something. But as far as sitting down and conversing with them, as far as having a back-and-forth conversation, never.

I talk with them all the time.

My wife thinks it's one of my more harmless fantasies. She knows that Little refers to Lucy, and Big refers to Caesar, and Mama Big refers to Caesar's mother. We mostly use those names when we are in a "Winter's Bone" mood.

Other times, the dogs are characters in "The Wire." Still other times, they're a prison gang, the Latin Pugs. The "original gangsters" were earlier pugs – Primo, Tia, Jorge and Chico.

My wife is familiar with all of this, but she is not a participant. She never talks about Little, or Big, or Richie R. Richmond. To her, they're just Lucy, Caesar and Richie.

Yet, if you were to have Mary and me call them, they might well run to Mary. In other words, I would not put too much emphasis on which person Tilly ran to.

Instead, if I were judge, I'd try a variation of Solomon's idea of splitting the baby. I'd say: "There are plenty of dogs that need homes. Why don't we flip a coin? The winner gets Tilly. The loser agrees to adopt a dog."

If both parties really love dogs — if this isn't an effort on the part of one to hurt the other — they would agree. And a dog that needs a home gets one.

If one party balks, no need to flip a coin. The other party gets Tilly.

Brilliant, right? I can't take credit for the idea. Lucy came up with it.

MAY 6, 2012

Bad breakup leaves dog in the middle

Mariana Sanchez and Tom Gray were childhood friends in Maplewood. Then their paths diverged. Tom, who was a couple of years older, dropped out of high school. Mariana went to college.

Years later, they reconnected and became a couple. Oddly enough, it was the high school dropout who seemed to be having the smoother ride. He had a steady job as the overnight cook at Tiffany's Diner on Manchester Road in downtown Maplewood.

Mariana, who had majored in marketing at Southeast Missouri University, was more or less bouncing around, looking for a career.

In the fall of 2009, she moved into Tom's apartment in Maplewood. In July 2010, they went to the St. Louis County pound and adopted a dog, a German shepherd-beagle mix named Tilly.

A few months later, Tom and Mariana broke up. Mariana moved out of Tom's apartment.

Last summer, she filed a lawsuit asking for custody of the dog.

The case was heard Thursday by Associate Circuit Judge Ellen Ribaudo.

I spoke with Mariana before the hearing began. She said Tilly was her dog. She said she signed the adoption papers. She said she took Tilly with her when she moved out of Tom's place.

She said she went out of town to a wedding last June and let Tom watch the dog. She said that when she came back, he wouldn't relinquish the dog. She said she called the Maplewood police, but they weren't much help. They all know him, she said with a shrug.

Not that it has anything to do with ownership of the dog, but I like a world in which the overnight cook at Tiffany's Diner is a man of influence.

I spoke briefly with Tom before the hearing began. He said Tilly was always his dog. He shook his head when I told him that Mariana had told me that she took Tilly when she moved out.

"That's just not true," he said.

Mariana was represented by Shannon Martinis and Philip Dennis. Martinis said she is new to the area and plans to specialize in animal cases.

Tom was represented by Richard Schwartz. He once represented Chuck Berry.

"I've never done an animal case," he said. "I'd feel better if this were a quarter horse."

The judge began the hearing by laying out the rules. The law considers the dog to be property, she said. The only issue is who is the rightful owner.

The first witness for Mariana was a "kennel specialist" who handled the adoption. She said she did not remember Tilly, Mariana or Tom, but she did recognize the adoption form that Mariana had signed.

Then Mariana took the stand and told the judge the same story she had told me earlier. She said again that she had taken Tilly when she moved out of Tom's apartment.

Tom's first witness was a man who lives in the building next to his apartment. The man testified that he had retired from the Marine Corps as a lieutenant colonel. He said he knew both Tom and Mariana.

Whose dog was it? I always thought it was Tom's dog, he said. Who had the dog when Mariana moved out? Tom did, he said. Was he sure of that? Yes. The two buildings share a yard and his dog plays with Tilly. He would notice if Tilly weren't there, he said.

Then Tom testified. He spoke slowly. He said he used to be the overnight cook at the diner. Now he's the manager.

He said he remembered picking Tilly out. She wasn't with the other dogs. She was standing alone. He liked that about her, he said.

Tom said that after he and Mariana broke up, he used to let Mariana come over and watch Tilly while he was at work. I was trying to make the best of a bad situation, he said.

But that didn't work out when his new girlfriend moved into his apartment, he said. Shortly thereafter, Mariana filed her lawsuit, he said.

What about the adoption form that Mariana had signed? Tom said he didn't write well. He probably let her handle the forms. He added that he had the receipts to show he paid for the dog.

Then Schwartz asked about education. Did he drop out of high school? Yes. Was he a special ed student? Yes. Did he have those records to give to the judge? Yes.

With that, Schwartz turned his client over for cross-examination.

How do you cross-examine such a witness without looking like a bully?

Dennis tried, but he didn't have much luck. Tom remained steady. Tilly was his dog, he said.

The judge has taken the case under advisement.

FEBRUARY 14, 2014

Visiting the girl in the poodle skirt

Herb Glazer never knew his benefactor's name. Nor what he looked like. Glazer figures he was a Jewish guy from St. Louis. In Glazer's mind, the unknown benefactor played the role of Cupid.

"I tell the grandkids if it wasn't for him, they wouldn't be here," he told me.

Glazer and his benefactor crossed paths in 1953 at the Army's Fort Belvoir in Virginia. Glazer was a working-class kid from St. Louis. He graduated from Soldan High School in 1951.

He was drafted in 1953, at the very end of the Korean War. After basic training, he was sent to Fort Belvoir for training as an engineer. He and most of the fellows from his company were told they were being sent to Germany. But when training ended and assignments were shouted out, five men in the company had mysteriously been added to the roster of men being sent to an Engineer Depot in Granite City.

All five were from the St. Louis area — Cohen, Glazer, Goldman, Greenberg and Weiss.

Nothing was ever explained, but Glazer figured that somebody — a Jewish company clerk? — had decided to give five Jewish kids from St. Louis a break and essentially send them home.

Oddly enough, only three of the five were Jewish. Weiss and Cohen were not.

So Glazer found himself stationed in Granite City. One day an old friend — actually a relative of a former girlfriend — called and asked if Glazer would take her cousin to a dance. The Soldan prom. Glazer was 21 and not so sure about this, but he agreed. He picked up his date. Her name was Brenda. She seemed nice. They were double-dating, and he and Brenda went to pick up the other couple.

The guy was waiting for his date at the foot of the stairs. Glazer and Brenda waited with him.

Finally, she came down the stairs. She was dressed in a white skirt with a black poodle embroidered on it. (Poodle skirts were big in those days.) She had a black-and-white top and a black ribbon tied around her neck. She was wearing black-and-white saddle shoes.

"She was a vision," Glazer said. Her name was Zelda, and Glazer was enchanted.

But he was also a gentleman, and that meant he danced with his own date. Then the band struck up "The Blue Tango," and neither Brenda nor Zelda's date knew how to do the tango. So for the first time, Glazer and Zelda danced.

At the table, they sat across from each other, and whenever Zelda would lean over to say something, she would put her hand up to her blouse to keep it from falling open. She was modest. Glazer was in love.

He called her the next Wednesday, and when he identified himself, she said, "What took you so long?"

From then on, they were a couple. Glazer got out of the Army soon after. He and Zelda decided to get married. As per the custom of the time, Glazer had to ask her father. His name was Abraham, and he was a quiet man who barely nodded to Glazer when they'd see each other. One day, Glazer blurted it out. He wanted to marry Zelda. Abraham said, "Well, I didn't think you hung around here because you liked the food."

With that blessing, they got married.

They were married in June 1956. By the way, Brenda was in the wedding party.

The Glazers had three children, a daughter and two sons. Herb worked a variety of jobs. Mostly, he was a salesman. He worked himself up to vice president of marketing for a big company, but he lost that job when the company was sold. He started over at 56. He eventually started a furniture repair and refinishing business.

Zelda was an artist. In October 1985, she was featured in American Artist magazine.

About seven years ago, Zelda began to have trouble remembering things. She'd ask something, and then a few minutes later, she'd repeat the question. The problem became acute enough that Zelda went to a doctor. She was diagnosed with Alzheimer's dementia.

For a couple of years, Herb was her caregiver, but that became too much. Five years ago, she moved to the West County Care Center. Herb visits daily. He speaks highly of the care Zelda receives.

I met him at the Care Center this week. He showed me a photo of her as a young woman. She was very pretty.

She is in a lockdown ward. Herb knows the combination, and we walked in. Zelda was in the hallway. She seemed to recognize Herb. "I love you," he said. "I love you," she said. It is a noisy ward, and not a place conducive to long visits. Herb told me his visits are always brief. He simply likes to see her, and let people know she has an advocate.

Herb and Zelda kissed lightly. "I love you," he said again, and then we left.

MAY 31, 2004

Upon closer look, soldier's letter raises unsettling questions

In January 1944, a woman wrote a letter to this newspaper. She said she had just received two letters, one from her husband, who was fighting overseas, and the second from one of his pals. She read the second letter first. Her husband's pal was writing to say how bad he felt that her husband had been killed. Then she read the letter from her husband. He wrote about how much he missed her: "I can hardly wait till I get back — if I ever do."

The woman talked a little about her husband. "He was born in a small town in Arkansas and he was an orphan since he was a small boy. He had no one but me." She said she was 29 and her husband was 34 and they had been married for two years. She said that she was pregnant with their first child. She signed her letter, Mrs. Earl Crumpton. The newspaper published her letter, and the letter from her husband. A reporter tried unsuccessfully to find her. Her letter had not carried a return address. Just "St. Louis."

Sixty years later, another reporter came across the letters and the story while doing some research. He showed them to me, and I decided to try to learn more. A colleague in the research department, Steve Bolhafner, got on the Internet and discovered that Sgt. Earl Crumpton of the Army Air Corps had been killed Jan. 5, 1944, and his remains were returned to this country in 1949. He was buried in a mass grave in Zachary Taylor National Cemetery in Kentucky. His birth date was given as March 6, 1916. That would mean that he was 27 when he was killed.

I called the cemetery. The man who answered the phone said they had no further information. I asked how reliable the birth date was. All we know is what they tell us, he said.

A check with City Hall showed no birth certificates issued in 1944 with Earl Crumpton as the father. No marriage licenses with the name Earl Crumpton, either, from 1941 through 1944.

I checked with the National Personnel Records Center here in Overland. Crumpton's records were destroyed in the fire of 1973. The only new information the center had was this: Crumpton had enlisted from Ogden, Kan.

I called information. There was one Crumpton listed in Ogden. Her name is Michelle. I called her and said I was trying to learn about an Earl Crumpton who was killed in 1944. "That's my uncle," she said. I'd like to find your cousin, I said. Earl's child. She said she didn't know anything about such a cousin and referred me to her uncle, Carl Crumpton. Earl was his brother. Carl is 79 and lives in Topeka, Kan.

Carl Crumpton told me about his family. He said he was the last survivor of 10 children. The family lived in Kansas. The father was a farmer and then a blacksmith. There were eight boys and two girls. Six of the eight boys were in the war. Two of them were killed: Earl, who died in a plane crash, and Elmer, who was killed in Germany six weeks before the war ended. Both of the girls' husbands fought, too, Carl said. None of that should come as a surprise, he added. Their father, Edward, fought in the Spanish-American War and their grandfather, Pinkney Crumpton, who lived with them, was a veteran of the Civil War. He was from South Carolina and fought for the South.

I thought about the letter from 60 years ago. "He was born in a small town in Arkansas and was an orphan since he was a small boy. He had no one but me."

Carl said he knew about the letter. Shortly after it was published, somebody from St. Louis sent it to them. Nobody in the family had heard that Earl was married, but whoever sent them the letter, knew who the woman was. One of Earl's sisters, Betty Jane, contacted the woman. The woman and Earl were not really married, Carl said. Betty Jane died last December, and so there was no way to learn the girlfriend's name, Carl said.

Was she really pregnant?

"We don't know," Carl said.

He said that Earl had girlfriends all over. He was tall and handsome, and a boxer of some renown. By the way, the cemetery had it right. Earl was 27 when he died.

"He was quite a rounder," Carl said. "He used to say, 'Why marry one and disappoint hundreds?' That was a favorite saying of his. He probably had girlfriends in London."

So the mystery of 60 years ago remains a mystery. We can only guess at parts of it. Did the woman in St. Louis make up that stuff about Earl being an orphan, or was that a line he used? Was he really in love with her, or was she one of many?

Personally, I like to think he was in love with her. The fact that he was a playboy in his youth — a rounder, as his brother put it — means little. The war could have changed his notions about what really matters in life. He must have talked about her. After all, his buddy wrote to her to tell her of his death. Perhaps the buddy realized that his letter would be the only way she'd learn of his death. The government did not notify girlfriends.

Carl told me he wrote a little something about Earl's death, and it was published in the newspaper in Topeka. It was about the personal effects that the government sent to their mother. One pair of shoes, one pair of shorts, one tie, one belt buckle, one handkerchief, two pairs of socks, two towels, two sewing kits, one soap box, one pair of wings and insignia and one very damaged wrist watch. That was it, Carl said. A few odds and ends to mark a life.

Not quite. In this instance, there was also a letter. Two letters, really. And an enduring mystery.

JANUARY 6, 1993

Woman befools 'regular guy'

If something seems too good to be true, it probably is. Why can't bachelors understand this?

Consider what happened to a fellow who is calling himself Larry. And let me digress here for an instant. This newspaper recently received a packet of letters. Actually, they were copies of letters. The man who sent us this packet wanted to embarrass a certain woman. However, because the story was also embarrassing to him, he had inked out his own name from these letters and had given himself the pseudonym of Larry. By holding the letters under a light, I was able to detect our hero's real name. But in an instance like this, male solidarity must count for something; so, Larry he shall remain. And now, back to our story.

Larry heard of an outfit called Romantic Pen Pals. For $10, RPP will send you a list of women who are interested in being pen pals. This is a very special list.

Accompanying each woman's name is a photograph and a short biography.

The photographs are, to say the least, revealing. The biographies are as scanty as the clothes.

There are several things that would make a rational man wonder about the legitimacy of the service.

In the first place, the women's names sound a bit phony. My favorite is April May, who hails from the St. Louis area. In the second place, all the addresses are P.O. boxes.

But most telling, I think, are the descriptions of the kind of men to whom these women are attracted.

Most legitimate such services — I think of the personals in the Riverfront Times, for instance — are rather depressing to a normal guy.

"Attractive female seeks slender, financially secure, professional man who enjoys opera and classical music."

But hey, that's life. That's the kind of man most women think they want until they meet a paunchy, paycheck-to-paycheck guy who enjoys watching sports on television.

The women in RPP have already reached that level of enlightenment. In fact, they're not even that particular. Here's a sample of their wish lists:

"Victoria O'Hara seeks man 21-55."

"Ali Magee needs a man."

"Liz Southern seeks steady guy."

"Pauline Gawron wants to live with a man, 20-65, not fussy."

Bearing in mind that all these women are attractive — and some are extremely attractive — a rational man might wonder how it is that these women, with their sights set so realistically low, have to advertise.

On the other hand, it's probably a kick to realize, "I qualify!"

So it was, apparently, with Larry. He selected an attractive 24-year-old whose mailing address was a post office box in Maryland Heights. Her name, supposedly, was Linda. She had no particular specifications for her dream guy. Her biography just said, "Needs love."

He wrote her a letter.

"I want to give you all the love you desire," he wrote.

He explained that he was quite a bit older than her, but looked 10 years younger than his real age. He said he was 5-foot-8, and weighed 155 pounds.

She responded quickly.

"You write an interesting letter, and you really are a very romantic guy, I can tell," she said. She threw in a couple of very personal asides — as he had in his letter — and then she asked for money.

"You might think about sending some money so I can send a few color photos," she suggested.

Larry sent her $5 with his next letter. He also suggested that they get together. Why write letters when they live so close?

Again, she responded quickly.

"I've never met a man like you before," she wrote. And yes, she wanted to meet him in person. She suggested a motel in Belleville. They could meet in the lounge. But she would need $50 in travel money.

That was fine with Larry. He wrote back to establish a time for the meeting. He did, however, have a question.

"Have you met many men since you placed your ad? I hope I'm your one and only," he wrote.

In her next letter, she assured him he was.

So he sent her $50 and went to the appointed motel at the appointed hour.

Linda did not show up!

Nor did she respond to any more letters, not even the one in which Larry threatened to take his story to the press.

Which, of course, he eventually did. I present it here as a cautionary tale.

Beware, bachelors, of attractive young women who pretend to be enlightened enough to want us normal guys.

Remember, they all think they want slender, financially secure professional men who enjoy opera and classical music.

We regular guys are an acquired taste.

JANUARY 19, 2003

German war bride, her soldier face latest battle together

Bob Lauenstein and his wife, Annemarie, are sharing a hospital room at St. Anthony's Medical Center. Letters and cards from grandchildren are taped to the walls. A scrapbook is on a table.

The scrapbook contains newspaper clippings from 1946. One of the stories is from the Los Angeles Times. It begins: "Pretty, blue-eyed Anna Heinke, 23, whose father died in a concentration camp, today received the first exit permit given to a German girl since the war to go to the U.S. to marry her American sweetheart." Yes, Annemarie was the first war bride to come here after President Truman signed the GI-Fiancee bill, which allowed American soldiers to bring their fiancees home. When Bob and Annemarie were married at the Trinity Lutheran church at Eighth and Soulard, a photographer from Life magazine took photos.

It helped, too, that the young couple had a nice story. Bob was part of an advance party for the 2nd Armored Division that entered Berlin in June 1945. The war had just ended. Berlin was in ruins. The advance party scoured the city, but could find no beer. Bob and another soldier took a jeep and drove to the Russian-controlled city of Dessau 70 miles away. The soldiers knew that a brewery had somehow survived the bombing that had destroyed most of that city.

The brewery was closed for the day when the two soldiers arrived. They sat on the bank of the Elba River and tried to figure out what to do. Two young German women were nearby. The soldiers heard them talking.

"Don't say too much," said Bob teasingly to the women. "I speak German."

He had studied German at Washington University. He had studied history, too, and journalism. The war had come along before he could finish college. He joined the Army, and landed in Normandy several days after D-Day.

The two young women were sisters. When they learned that the Americans needed a place to spend the night, they invited them home. They lived with their mother. Their father had been arrested on Christmas Eve of 1943 and charged with saying negative things about Hitler. His distaste for the Nazis was well-known. He died in prison.

The soldiers picked up their beer in the morning and returned to Berlin. The beer run became a weekly event, and before long, Bob and Annemarie were in love.

In December 1945, the battalion received orders back to the states. Bob broke the news to Annemarie.

"I thought you might want to stay here and marry me," she said.

"That's exactly what I want to do," he said.

He received permission to get his discharge in Berlin. He got a job as a translator. Then in November 1946, they came to St. Louis.

Bob eventually became an executive with a steel company. He and his wife had two children. The years rolled along. The couple celebrated their 56th anniversary in November.

Last month, Annemarie came down with pneumonia. She was admitted to St. Anthony's. The doctors said she might not make it. She was put on a ventilator.

As Bob sat in the waiting room outside of intensive care, he told his daughter, Ingrid, that he had a lump on his collarbone. She told him he should have it checked out, and he did. A week before Christmas, he learned he had end-stage cancer. The doctor said he had, maybe, four months to live.

He did not want to tell his wife until she was a little stronger. Unfortunately, Bob's condition deteriorated, and he was rushed to St. Luke's Hospital. The end could come any day, the doctor said.

So he would have to tell his wife by phone. They would never see each other again.

But doctors and administrators at the two hospitals came up with a plan. Bob was transferred to St. Anthony's last Saturday. They gave him a bed in his wife's room, and they moved the beds together so Bob and Annemarie could hold hands.

They both seem stronger now.

"Just having him here with me is good," said Annemarie. Bob smiled.

JANUARY 26, 2003

Shared lives, cherished memories and perfect endings

I visited Bob and Annemarie Lauenstein on Jan. 17, and wrote about them for last Sunday's paper.

Their daughter, Ingrid, had already told me their story. They met in Germany in 1945. Bob was an American soldier. Annemarie was a German girl. They fell in love, and Bob stayed in Germany after his discharge. When President Harry S Truman signed the bill authorizing GIs and former soldiers to bring their German fiancees to this country, Bob and Annemarie hopped on a plane and flew to New York, and then to St. Louis. Because Annemarie was the first of the German war brides to come to this country, the Lauensteins got a ton of publicity. Throw in the fact that Bob was a good storyteller, and Annemarie's father had died in a Nazi prison, and it's easy to see why the press really took to the couple.

Then life settled down, and years went by. Last month, Annemarie got pneumonia. She nearly died. Ingrid flew in from North Carolina to be with her mother. While she and her father were in the waiting room of the intensive care unit at St. Anthony's Medical Center, he mentioned to his daughter that he had a lump on his collarbone. Get that checked out, Dad, she said. He did, and it turned out to be cancer. He was given four months to live. He did not want to tell his wife until she regained her strength, but he took a sudden turn for the worse, and was rushed to St. Luke's Hospital. He was told he had days to live, not months. Maybe hours.

He was going to have to tell his wife by phone.

But doctors and administrators at the two hospitals got together, and Bob was transferred to St. Anthony's, and put in his wife's room.

Both Bob and Annemarie were in good spirits when I visited. Annemarie was no longer on a ventilator. Bob seemed strong, and was very candid about his condition.

"I'm terminal," he told me.

Still, he had no trouble telling the old stories one last time. How he met his wife on the banks of the Elbe River. How he eventually smuggled her to Berlin behind some cases of beer. (The authorities were hoping to prevent a huge influx of refugees into the city.) How he told her that his unit was about to ship home, and she suggested he stay in Germany. Which he did.

Bob was 80 as he told these stories, but the young man was not far from the surface. It was easy to see him as a handsome, resourceful GI. And if a fellow could be described as robust on his death bed, that description could have fit Bob. Perhaps the telling of the stories gave him strength, as if the memories were a time machine of sorts. Perhaps that is exactly what they are. At any rate, he talked effortlessly, and I felt privileged to listen. There are times when newspapering is the best of trades.

Annemarie did more listening than talking during my visit. But what a life she has lived. The Gestapo came for her father on a Christmas Eve, she told me. He was accused of anti-Hitler utterances. This had to do with a poem, she said. He was given a three-year sentence, and he died in prison. Sometime after his arrest, their house was hit in an allied bombing raid, and she and her sister and mother moved to another place. It was bombed, too.

"Some of her hair had been burnt off when I met her," Bob said.

He was still fine Saturday when the early edition of the newspaper came out. Ingrid brought him a copy. He liked the story. He lost consciousness Sunday, and he died Monday. He did not seem to be in any pain, Ingrid said, and he was surrounded by love. His daughter cradled his head in her arms. It's all right to leave, she said. It sounded like a perfect ending to a good life.

And it must have been a good life because I received a number of messages from people who had known him. A kind man, somebody said. A wonderful sense of humor, somebody else said.

After Annemarie recuperates, she will live with her daughter and grandchildren in North Carolina.

AUGUST 23, 1985

Orchestrating personal ads

If you were to call me and say that you were having trouble meeting a person of the opposite sex, I would transfer you to Martha Carr, a colleague of mine who writes about that kind of thing. She would probably tell you to become active in the community and meet people that way.

If you were to reject that advice — if you become active in the community, you'd meet somebody who's active in the community, and then you'd spend the rest of your life getting dragged to meetings — I'd be sympathetic, but I still wouldn't help you. I'm not in the business of playing Cupid.

But every now and then, along comes a situation in which Cupid needs a shove. Such a situation is unfolding right now.

Leonard Smith is looking for a woman.

On the surface, that's no big deal. Smith is single. He's a healthy 64-year-old man. He knows that love can give meaning to a man's life.

Smith works as a security guard at the Shell Building in downtown St. Louis. That is not a good job for meeting women. Most of the women who go past his station are rushing around on business. Besides, Smith works the 4 to 11 shift, and the building is closed for most of that period.

So Smith is trying another route. He is responding to the personal ads in a free weekly newspaper that circulates downtown.

Maybe you've seen those ads. The ads make it clear that this city is filled with attractive, professional, slim, affectionate, fun-loving women who wish to meet a nonsmoker.

Smith smokes a pack of cigarettes a day. He's ineligible to answer most of the ads. And many of the attractive, professional, affectionate women are looking for someone who is, as they say in their ads, financially secure.

Smith does not even own a car.

Still, he persists. He answers the ads that seem most reasonable. He answered two last week.

One was from a "big beautiful woman who has a great deal to offer and just happens to be obese."

Another was from a woman who enjoys baseball games and bowling and is emotionally fit.

Both of those women sounded appealing to Smith. He wrote them each a letter. He explained that he enjoyed flea markets and country and Western music. He said he loved to cook. He described himself as gentle, loving and caring. He said he drank two cans of beer a day and smoked a pack of cigarettes.

Smith did not pretend to be a matinee idol. He didn't say he was good-looking or well-built. Except for noting his height (5 feet 10), the color of his hair (brown) and the color of his eyes (blue), the only mention he made of his appearance concerned his tattoos. He has 15 tattoos, he said, seven on one arm, eight on the other.

All in all, the letters were straightforward and honest. But as of the middle of this week, neither woman had responded.

Maybe they got the wrong impression from the letters. Maybe they thought Smith sounded dull or unromantic. They probably did not realize that Smith is a man willing to lose everything for love. And he is.

The last time he went looking for love in the classifieds, it cost him his job.

He was working for a security guard company. He was stationed, more or less permanently, at Powell Hall. The year was 1979.

He wrote a personal ad, and the paper published it. It was a straightforward ad. A gentle and caring man wanted to meet a woman. Meet me at the guard station at Powell Hall any night the Symphony is playing, the letter said. It was signed Leonard S.

Unfortunately for Leonard Smith, some women put two and two together and came up with five. They thought that the only caring and gentle Leonard S. at Powell Hall was Leonard Slatkin. He is the conductor of the Symphony.

Perhaps some of those women complained. Perhaps Slatkin complained. It doesn't matter who complained.

What matters is that Smith got fired. Powell Hall is only big enough for one

Leonard S.

Before getting fired, though, Smith did meet a woman at the guard station. Her name was Lucille, and she and Smith lived together for four years, until Lucille died two years ago.

So Smith says he is glad he put the ad in. If you believe in love, which Smith obviously does, you know that love is more important than a job.

What a shame that such a romantic attitude did not come through in Smith's letters. If it had, I'm sure at least one of the women would have answered him by now.

I think he could make some woman happy, even though his last name isn't Slatkin.

NOVEMBER 22, 2000

Couple believes good future is near after living tough pasts

Sherry works the morning shift at a fast-food restaurant in St. Louis. She works at the grill, frying this and frying that.

She's 41 years old, so she's a bit older than most of her colleagues. That's fine with Sherry. She's like most people. You have work, and then you have the parallel universe of life. In Sherry's parallel universe, she has a fiance. I met him once. It was a very brief meeting, and he seemed shy. Sherry told me he suffers from a social phobia. She defined it as a fear of being around people. Whatever the medical definition is, it's enough to get him a small disability check. He gets $429 a month.

Perhaps Sherry could get a disability check. She says she has a bipolar condition and suffers from depression and attention deficit disorder. On the other hand, she is able to function in society. She has a GED. She even enrolled at a local community college once. She dropped all of her classes except for English composition. She got an A in that class. Plus, of course, she is capable of holding a job.

Not that life is easy. She went to jail once. It was, she said, sort of a misunderstanding. She said she found a bag at the airport. The bag was filled with camera equipment. She needed some money, so she took some of the equipment to a pawn shop. A short time later, the police showed up at her apartment. She was charged with felony theft, but she said she didn't really steal anything. The bag was just sitting there. She found it. She didn't steal it. Wouldn't she have tried to fence it on the street if she thought she had stolen it? Instead, she went to a pawn shop and used her own name. Still, she pleaded guilty and got probation.

Sometime later, she got messed up with drugs and was arrested for selling crack cocaine. She wasn't really selling it, she said. This guy asked if she could get him $20 worth of crack, and she said, sure, and she got it for him. That's a sale? There was no profit. But that was enough to get her probation revoked on the earlier theft conviction. She did a total of about seven months.

She was sent to a drug and alcohol treatment center in Farmington. She met a guy there and, when she finished treatment, went to live with him and his mother near there. The three of them lived in a trailer, and things were pretty good. She got a factory job. She was a seamstress. About the time the romance had run its course with the fellow from the treatment center, she met another guy and moved into his trailer. She said they got engaged but it didn't work out because he was violent and still in love with his ex-wife.

At any rate, she ended up back here. She met her fiance about nine months ago. At the time, she wasn't working, and his disability check wasn't enough to make a deposit on an apartment or pay first and last month's rent, so they lived on the streets.

Sherry and her fiance are happy — grateful, actually — to accept meals from the churches and missions that provide them, but they try not to spend any nights in the various shelters. They prefer the streets.

Not too long ago, they found a nice place. Pretty nice, anyway. It's the shell of a place that burned down. At night, they take a roll of toilet paper, soak it in rubbing alcohol and put it in a coffee can. Then they light it. It's a good clean burn, Sherry said.

While she's at work, her fiance moves around. Sometimes he walks. Sometimes he rides. He has a monthly bus pass, so sometimes he gets on a bus and just rides and rides. Apparently, the people on the bus don't bother him.

Now that Sherry is working, she figures it won't be long before she and her fiance have enough cash for an apartment. How long? Certainly by Christmas.

In the meantime, the little fire in the coffee can puts out a bit of heat. Not much, but enough. Then the morning comes, and Sherry goes to the fast-food restaurant to stand by the warm grill.

OCTOBER 12, 1997

Public opinion rules in favor of prison romance

The Court of Public Opinion is now in session, the Honorable William McClellan presiding.

We have before us today a love story. A couple is getting married later this month. Our question is this: Should the bride be allowed to visit the groom after the wedding? Our bride is Jeri Renee LeGrand. She is engaged to David Leisure.

The wedding is scheduled for Oct. 23. There will be no honeymoon, and that's fine with this court, but prison authorities won't let Leisure put LeGrand on his visiting list.

Leisure is at Potosi Correctional Center. He is under two death sentences.

Students of St. Louis history remember Leisure. He was, and is, Paul Leisure's nephew and Anthony Leisure's cousin, and thus he was part of the so-called Leisure Gang that warred with the Michaels family in the early '80s for control of the St. Louis mob, such as it was.

There's no way to sugarcoat car-bombings — and this court has no intention of so doing — but there was something almost endearing about the Leisure Gang. There was a Wile E. Coyote touch to the gang. They were headquartered at the LN&P towing company, and of course the feds bugged the place, and the conversations were right out of the cartoons. In one exchange, one of the guys wistfully suggested climbing onto the roof of one of their enemies and lowering sticks of dynamite down the chimney into the fireplace.

That would show everybody who's smart!

David, incidentally, was never considered one of the brighter guys in the gang.

Before he hit the big time with the car-bombings, he was always getting busted for burglaries. In fact, during the first of his two car-bombing trials, his attorney argued that he had the intellect of an 11-year-old. He shouldn't be held fully accountable for his actions, his attorney said.

Of course, that was his attorney talking. For all this court knows, the attorney was just playing an angle. It could be that David is really smart.

LeGrand thinks he's a very nice guy.

She met David about 20 years ago, before all the heavy troubles started. As she tells the story, she was dating one of David's cousins, a fellow who later had his own legal problems but was not connected to the Leisure Gang.

At any rate, she got to know David, and when he found himself in City Jail awaiting his trials on the two murder charges, she visited him. He was just like she remembered. Very nice.

She had, by the way, a few problems of her own. Mostly these problems had to do with writing checks on accounts that had been closed. There were more than a couple of these charges, and she eventually got federal and state time.

Which is the crux of her problem.

No matter whom you believe — and we'll get to that in a minute — she would not have used a fake identification and an alias to visit David in Potosi if she didn't have a record.

You see, her relationship with David eventually evolved into something more serious than friendship. Last summer, she began visiting him at Potosi on a very regular basis. Ten times a month, hours at a time.

She did it under an assumed name.

"I made the mistake of telling another inmate's wife my business. That was my mistake," she said. "Somebody dropped a dime on me."

She says she only used the alias because the prison authorities wouldn't put her on the visiting list because of her record. The prison authorities say they're flexible about people with criminal records visiting the prison, and the authorities contend that LeGrand assumed she couldn't visit because of her record and that she used a false name and identification when she didn't even have to. But as long as she did, she's no longer trusted.

Consequently, her visiting privileges have been suspended.

The law says the state has to let an inmate get married if he and his fiancee meet the legal requirements of the county in which the prison is situated. But there is no court ruling that says the prison has to let the wife visit.

Hence, the Court of Public Opinion has been convened.

Let's first deal with the question of LeGrand's record. It shouldn't stop her from visiting Potosi. After all, most of the inmates are in there for murder. I don't think a bad-check writer is going to be much of a bad influence.

The alias thing is a bit stickier. That was a bad thing, a foolish thing.

But people in love always do foolish things. This court is always willing to make allowances for love.

As a wedding present, prison authorities ought to relent. LeGrand should be allowed to visit her husband.

APRIL 1, 1998

'War bride' seeks cozy bungalow for love of her life

The letter found its way to Places for People, an agency on Lindell Boulevard. Quite obviously, the woman who wrote the letter did not know anything about the agency, which serves the mentally ill.

Indeed, the writer seemed to know only the name of the agency, and she was, it turns out, looking for a place for people. Hopefully, a bungalow with a garden.

The woman, Elisha Houpt, lives in England. She is 78 years old.

According to her letter, she met her husband, who is 92, when he served with the U.S. Army Air Corps in England.

"We met in 1944," she wrote. "He had to go home at the end of the war. I couldn't go with him then. But we never forgot each other. In 1987, I searched for him. I found him. In January of 1990, we married."

They moved to England. Now he is ill. His memory is failing.

"That doesn't matter," the letter continued. "He knows me, and I still have him."

She wants to bring her husband to Missouri, Elisha Houpt wrote, because Missouri is his home. In fact, some days he thinks he's there now.

"He thinks he is in Joplin. I go along with him. I do not contradict," she wrote.

The director of Places for People is Francie Broderick. She is something of a romantic.

"This woman is 78 years old, and she's willing to uproot herself for her husband," Broderick told me.

She called information in England, but apparently the Houpts do not have a telephone.

So Broderick wrote Elisha a letter. While she awaits a response, she sent me a copy of Elisha's letter.

It was, I thought, like something out of a movie.

According to the letter, D.J. Houpt grew up in Joplin. He lived with his mother prior to the war.

He was not a young man when he left his mother. In 1944, the year he met Elisha, he was 38.

She was 24.

Exactly what he did in the Army Air Corps is unclear. Elisha mentioned a friend of hers who married a pilot, and now lives in Texas. Perhaps Houpt was also a pilot.

You could fill in that part of the script yourself.

Also this part — "He had to go home at the end of the war. I couldn't go with him then."

The wording certainly suggests that he asked her to go with him, so for the purpose of our script, let's assume that he did. She couldn't. Family obligations? Family objections? Maybe a previous commitment to some other young man?

At any rate, she couldn't go.

Decades passed.

Forty-two years after he left England, she decided to try to find him. At the time of this momentous decision, she was 66. She knew that if he were alive, he'd be 79.

She did find him. Perhaps it's because he was still in Joplin. Was he a widower?

Or had he gone home, a man hitting 40, and gone back to his mother?

If so — and that's the way my script would have it — the whole experience in England must have seemed like a dream. The war, the girl, the rejected proposal. It was a movie about somebody else's life.

And then she came back from across the great divide of the years.

They have been married now for eight years. Perhaps they wonder, sometimes, about the years they missed.

But perhaps not. The letter makes it sound like they live very much in the present.

"Life is so precious to us," Elisha wrote.

In a wistful passage, she described the kind of place in Missouri she's looking for.

"I'd prefer a bungalow. He would potter about in the garden," she wrote.

Broderick knows that this request is well beyond the parameters of Places for People. There is, in all likelihood, nothing she can do.

But still, she read the letter and was touched.

"He is a wonderful, remarkable man," Elisha wrote, and she sounded not so much like a 78-year-old woman, but more like a 24-year-old girl.

APRIL 6, 1998

Life is often better than the movies, in romance and in fact

Late last month, Francie Broderick, the director of Places for People, got a letter from Dorothy Joy Houpt of England. She said she was 78 years old, and she was looking for a bungalow with a small garden.

She explained that her husband was from Missouri. He was 92 and in failing health, and it would probably do him good to return home. She said that they had met in England during the war. She was 24. He was 38. "He had to go home at the end of the war. I couldn't go with him then. But we never forgot each other. In 1987, I searched for him. I found him. In January of 1990, we married," Houpt wrote.

Broderick knows that I am partial to love stories, and she sent the letter to me. I wrote about it last week. It's like a movie script, I suggested. And I wondered what the story was behind the simple statement — "I couldn't go with him then."

The day the column appeared, I got a call from a friend in Greenville, Ill.

"The man in your story just died," my friend said. "His nephew lives next door to me."

So I called the nephew. His name is Leo Houpt.

He confirmed that his uncle had died in England a week or so ago. He told me a little about his uncle.

Ralph was the youngest of six kids. He grew up in a farmhouse southwest of Joplin, Mo. He loved the outdoors. He once trapped a white squirrel and kept it for a pet. The family didn't have much money, and the father was gone a good deal of the time.

"The father had sand in his shoes," Leo said. "That was the expression they used."

Ralph was in his late 30s and single when he was drafted. He went into the Army Air Corps.

"He was an enlisted man, but somehow he got involved in flying. We could never get much out of him about that. I heard he was badly wounded on one flight over Germany."

As far as the romance was concerned, Leo said he didn't know much.

"I met Joy about a year ago," Leo said. "They flew to the states for a visit. I thought she was a real pretty girl, really perky, too."

He then suggested that I call his cousin, Edna Sander. She lives in Kansas and is pretty much the family historian.

Edna knew the whole story.

Ralph and Joy did fall in love in 1944. At the time, Joy was married, but her husband had vanished somewhere in the south Pacific. She figured he was dead.

He wasn't. When she found out he was alive, that was the end of the romance with Ralph. Honor and obligation and all of that.

Ralph came home and worked as a merchant seaman. Then he got a job with the highway department in New Jersey. He got married. He and his wife never had any children.

In 1987, Joy's husband died, and she wrote a letter to a newspaper in Kansas, where she thought Ralph might have relatives. I'm looking for a Ralph Houpt who served in England during the war, she wrote.

A cousin saw the letter and called Edna.

"I wrote to Joy and explained that Ralph was married, but his wife was ill. Any contact would have to wait," Edna told me.

In 1990, Ralph's wife died, and Edna told him about the letter.

He wrote to Joy. She immediately came to the states, and they were married. They lived in Newfoundland until he had a stroke in 1995. Then she took him back to England.

I asked Edna if she thought that Ralph and Joy had always been in love, even though they had had no contact for more than 40 years.

"I have no doubt about that," she told me. "My uncle was a very gentle, very caring man. It's easy to see how you wouldn't forget him."

I hung up and went back and read again the letter that Joy had sent Broderick.

"He is a wonderful, remarkable man," Joy had written. "Life is so precious to us."

All those years apart. A romance that seemed destined not to be.

Then, at the very end, eight years together. No wonder life seemed so precious to them.

It should be a movie.

DECEMBER 1, 1999

Couple embraced the world after finding each other

In 1925, a fire caused heavy damage at St. Joseph's Catholic Church in Clayton. Adolph Gutman, a Jewish businessman who owned a nearby department store, delivered a large check to the priest. I think Clayton needs a Catholic church, Gutman said.

If the church can ever do anything for you, said Father Victor Stepka. The businessman game him a quizzical look.

If your kids want to get married at the church, there is always a place for them, said the priest. Both men laughed.

That is the story that has been handed down. Handed down and nearly forgotten until this summer, when David Gutman, Adolph's grandson, married Susie Ziervogel at St. Joseph's.

David was 56. Susie was 40. It was the first marriage for each.

Before Susie met David, she was doing OK. She worked at a fast-food restaurant for eight years, and then she got a job at a grocery store as a bagger. A very nice job.

Plus, she was living alone.

So, she had reason to feel good about herself. She had been a Special School District student in the days before mainstreaming came into vogue. As a developmentally disabled kid, she had gone to school with other developmentally disabled kids. When she was 17, she went to Columbia, Mo., to live in a group home for developmentally disabled people. When she returned to St. Louis three years later, she enrolled in a Life Skills program. As its name suggests, its goal is to teach people how to live independently.

Which is exactly what Susie was doing. Working and living alone.

She was blessed with a strong support system. A mother, a stepfather, a father, siblings, an extended family. But still, she was making it alone. That meant a lot to her.

David was out in the world, too. He lived with his stepmother, but he worked at the St. Louis County Election Board. He started working there in 1966. He hardly ever missed a day. As of last week, he had accumulated 1,897.9 hours of sick time. It is, people say, an unofficial record.

He was a cheerful sort, even before he met Susie. He'd show up every morning with a bag of pretzels, or a box of bagels. Cheerful and happy, but sheltered. Didn't get out much. Absolutely unstylish. Went from home to work, and work to home. His only diversion was bowling.

Susie's mother, Susan Davenport, had heard about David. Neighbors of hers were related to him, and she had heard that he was a very nice man, and she found herself wishing that Susie and he could meet. Actually, David and his stepmother lived quite close to Susan and her husband, Jack.

But Susan didn't do anything until April 1997, when she heard from her friends that David's stepmother had died. Susan stopped by to offer her condolences.

He was nice, and soon they were talking, and he mentioned that he liked to bowl, and Susan asked him when and where he bowled, and she said, maybe my daughter and I will come out to watch you, and he said that would be fine.

So that's how Susie and David met. At a bowling alley.

I talked to Susie this week, and I asked how long it took her to realize that David was Mr. Right. She laughed.

"Second frame," she said. "Right away."

David was just as smitten. David and Susie became inseparable.

Susie was like a teenager, so much in love. David was changed, too. For one thing, he was going out. Work was still important, but now there were other things, as well. He was going to restaurants. He was planning trips. He even became a little conscious of his clothes. Most noticeably, he started wearing dark socks.

David and Susie were married this past July. July 10, to be exact. Father Jerry Kleba of St. Joseph's and Rabbi Joseph Rosenbloom of Temple Emanuel co-officiated.

"These were two people who had thought they would never find someone," Father Kleba said. "And then to find each other. They were just aglow. We are all broken and fragile people, but these two people came together to make a perfect whole."

Rabbi Rosenbloom said, "If you were writing a novel, you couldn't do better than this."

In fact, the emotions were so high that the wedding party had a difficult time getting through the rehearsal. When it came time for David to acknowledge his love, he was crying.

Father Kleba was prepared for the actual service. As the ceremony approached the point when the bride and groom would have to speak, the priest said, "In the 157-year history of this church, we have had a number of double-ring ceremonies. This is our first double-hankie ceremony."

Then he pulled out two handkerchiefs, and handed one to Susie and one to David.

The couple honeymooned at Disney World.

They were soon taking other trips. Kansas City, Chicago, even Quebec. So many places to see now that they each had somebody with whom to see these places.

Last Saturday, they went to a movie. The weather was bad, and they came out into the cold, and maybe the cold triggered David's asthma attack, but he suddenly fell to his knees in the snow.

"Are you all right?" asked his wife.

He looked up at her, and said, "I love you, Susie, and I always will," and then he fell headfirst into the snow.

"I love you, too, David," said Susie.

As Rabbi Rosenbloom prepared the eulogy, he decided he would be directing his remarks to Susie. He took his pen and scratched out some thoughts.

"Your loss is tragic," he wrote. "A good man, a wonderful relationship, cut off all too soon, too suddenly – but your love, your memories, will live on."

Yes, that was the tone he wanted.

His eulogy went over well, and Susie understood exactly what the rabbi meant. A love story is never judged by its length.

SEPTEMBER 18, 1992

Love means never dwelling on his past

The waiter brought a bottle of champagne to the table. The woman looked at the champagne, looked at her boyfriend.

He bounced out of his chair, moved to his girlfriend's side of the table and sank to his knees. "I love you with all my heart. Will you marry me?" he asked.

She said yes.

Her name is Marcia Darling, and she works in the clerk's office at the Federal Courthouse in St. Louis. She's a pretty woman, and it's not at all surprising that she has gotten engaged to a lawyer.

Sort of a lawyer, anyway.

Her fiance is Gregory Scher. For many years, he has been considered one of the finest jailhouse lawyers in the state of Missouri.

He recently got out of prison after doing nine years of a 15-year sentence for fraudulently obtaining an airplane. What a fine case that was. Scher, a licensed pilot, posed as an aide to then-Sen. Tom Eagleton, and rented a jet to take him and several friends to Florida for a space shuttle launch.

Fifteen years seemed a bit steep for the crime.

And considering that most people do a third of their time, nine years seemed like a lot of time for a 15-year sentence.

But part of the blame belonged to Scher. If he were the sort of guy who could sit back and quietly do time, he'd have been out long ago. But Scher is not that sort of guy. He likes to have fun.

So some of his time he kept busy doing humorous, albeit larcenous, things. My favorite was when he wrote a letter to a Canadian boot company. He introduced himself as Dr. Gregory Scher, chairman and chief executive officer of the World Warbird Federation. He explained that his annual trip to the South Pole would be covered by cable television, and he stated that he would be willing to plug the company's boots if the company would send him a pair.

This scam, incidentally, was mentioned by an assistant attorney general a couple of years ago in an effort to discredit Scher.

The reason the attorney general's office has been so eager to discredit Scher was that his favorite activity in prison had to do with lawsuits. He filed a bunch of them, and he won more than a few.

Naturally, this did not endear him to state officials.

But it did win him a wide following in the federal courthouse.

Although his lawsuits were serious business, Scher was an absolute comedian on the witness stand.

"Who did you sit next to at the space shuttle launch?" a hostile attorney asked him once.

"I don't recall," said Scher.

The attorney strutted around as if he had caught Scher in a terrible lie.

"Didn't you once testify that you sat next to George Bush?" the attorney finally asked.

"Maybe I did sit next to him," replied Scher. "But really, George Bush is a very forgettable fellow."

Even the judge laughed.

This exchange took place during the trial involving the lawsuit of a convict named Robert Iron Eyes. The suit, prepared by Scher, alleged that Iron Eyes, a native American, needed for religious reasons to have his hair longer than prison regulations allowed.

It was during this trial, several years ago, that Darling first noticed Scher.

"All the women in the courthouse were crazy about him," she recalls.

She saw him, from afar, at several other trials. Then, this summer, he walked into the clerk's office. He had just been released from prison and sent to a halfway house. He was filing a temporary restraining order asking that the state release him outright.

The temporary restraining order never went anywhere, but a romance developed.

His background might be questionable — can a con man ever be trusted? — but there's no denying that Scher is fun.

"He is exciting," Darling told me after they had started to date.

Tuesday night, I met Darling and Scher at Ramon's Jalapeno in downtown Clayton.

"He eats in such big bites," said Darling.

"They used to club us if we didn't hurry," said Scher.

Except for his big bites, Scher seemed the very image of success. He said he was the jet operations manager and sales coordinator for Air Spirit Aviation. He had a new minivan in the parking lot, new credit cards in his wallet.

After Darling accepted Scher's proposal, Bryant Pittman joined us at the table. He's a salad and dessert chef at the restaurant, and a pal of Scher's from prison.

"He's an amazing guy," said Pittman.

He is all of that, I said.

"Life is good," said Scher.

Then he laughed, obviously pleased with the world, and poured himself another glass of champagne.

APRIL 9, 2012

Life can be trying – as court will testify

If you believe Alfred Lord Tennyson, this is the time of year a young's man fancy lightly turns to thoughts of love.

I thought about that when a young couple came into the courthouse the other day to get married. The young man was wearing a suit and the bride was wearing a wedding dress.

People stared at them. Not so much because they were getting married, but because they were so dressed up. People don't dress up much, anymore.

People used to dress up for all sorts of things. They would dress up to go on an airplane. They would dress up for sporting events. Check out some of the news footage from 40 years ago. Men wore suits to baseball games.

Certainly, people used to dress up to go to court. Especially defendants. The whole idea was to look like a wholesome citizen. Defendants don't seem to care about that, anymore.

I remember attending a probation revocation in which the defendant wore a T-shirt that said, "Public Enemy Number One." It turns out that was the name of a band, but still, there was a good chance the judge didn't know that. How do you not revoke probation for a guy with that T-shirt?

Actually, the judge did not.

At any rate, the happy young couple went through the metal detector and proceeded up the escalator.

I thought briefly of following them, but I was headed to a trial.

Good thing, too. Let them get married quietly. I'm not sure a newspaper story is good luck.

Years ago, I wrote a story about two people who fell in love while working together at the Popeye's Famous Fried Chicken store on North Kingshighway. They moved in together, and then planned a big church wedding. The young woman's uncle was a pastor, and he was going to preside.

The young woman got pregnant, but that was fine with everybody. The wedding was going to beat the arrival of the baby, but barely.

On the morning of the wedding, the young woman went into labor. The young man called her uncle and asked him to meet them at the hospital and perform the ceremony before the baby was born.

The pastor agreed, but his van broke down at Kingshighway and Oakland. He called a friend who runs a towing and car repair service out of his home. He agreed to tow the van to the hospital.

He and the reverend rushed into the hospital. The tow truck driver stayed in the waiting area while the pastor went into the delivery room. He was going to have a nurse be the witness, but the nurse was too busy doing medical things, so the pastor sent the groom into the waiting area to get the tow truck driver.

The young woman said "I do" between contractions, and she was married by the time the baby arrived.

Several years later, I called the young woman. I ought to do a follow-up, I said.

We're divorced, she said.

So the young couple at the courthouse ought to be glad I had other plans that morning.

The trial I was watching had a long break, so I wandered around the courthouse. I shared an elevator with two lawyers. They seemed like friends, but they were on opposite sides of a divorce case.

"I've got to tell you. There's not much middle ground here," said one.

"Oh, great. The kind of case I love. No money. No middle ground," said the other.

Still killing time, I walked down a hallway until I saw something going on in one of the courtrooms. I walked in and took a seat.

A young woman was on the witness stand. Apparently, she was trying to get a protective order. A young man sat at the defense table. He was shaking his head in denial as the young woman testified.

She said something to the effect that most of the time their love life was not consensual.

The young man's lawyer, a woman, snapped at her. Exactly what did you mean by not consensual?

Most of the time it's just to keep the peace, the young woman said.

The lawyer snapped again. But you were voluntarily keeping the peace. You were consenting to do that. Isn't that correct?

The young woman shrugged. The young man continued to shake his head. The bailiff looked as if he'd heard variations of this sad song before.

I left the courtroom and went back to the trial I'd been watching.

If Tennyson ever hung around the courthouse, he probably just stayed by the metal detector. It's more romantic than the courtrooms.

MARCH 14, 1988

All-American wife for death-row killer

In these enlightened times it is considered sexist for a reporter to describe a woman as attractive, but that's one of the odd things about Lynn Smith. She is attractive. Also odd is the fact that she's intelligent.

I had talked to her a couple of times, but she was just a voice on the phone. Now here she was, standing at my desk. She's 40ish and blond. Her style could be described as All-American, Donna Reedish, the woman next door.

She's married to Gerald Smith, who resides on death row in the Missouri State Prison in Jefferson City.

Gerald Smith and I have talked a few times, too, always by phone. Smith is an interesting fellow, to say the least.

He was convicted of murdering a former girlfriend a few years ago. On the surface, it didn't seem like a great death-penalty case. A person could make a good argument that it was a crime of passion. Furthermore, a state psychiatrist and a state psychologist were prepared to testify that Smith was incapable of premeditation.

But shortly before his trial, Smith wrote a letter to a newspaper. It was a damning letter. He said he had planned the murder. You bet it was premeditated, he said. He said he had a gun, but chose to beat his victim because he wanted her to suffer. He said he enjoyed killing, and would kill again if he were ever released.

Suddenly, it was a good death-sentence case, and the death sentence is what Smith got.

Unlike most fellows who fade from the public view once they hit the row, Smith kept making news. He said he wanted to be executed. He fought his attorney, who was trying to appeal the case.

Then, as if to cement his position, he was accused of stabbing another inmate to death.

It was shortly after the stabbing that Lynn Short met Gerald Smith.

She was from California, and she had a friend who corresponded with inmates. The friend asked her to write a letter to Smith, and pretty soon they were exchanging letters.

She says his letters were sensitive and humorous, and were never complaining.

When Smith's attorney was trying to urge his client to reconsider his refusal to allow an appeal, the attorney got in touch with Lynn Short. Maybe he'll listen to you, the lawyer said.

So she flew in from California, went to the prison and met Smith.

It was frightening, she says. She was put in a small room while the guards went to get Smith. She could trace Smith's progress by listening to the guards shouting.

"Clear the floor! Smith on the floor!"

In addition to the shouting, metal doors clanked as they were opened and shut.

She met Smith in these bizarre circumstances in April of 1986. Ten months later, they were married in the prison's waiting room. By that time, Smith no longer wanted to die.

A couple of months after the marriage, Smith went to trial for the murder of the inmate on death row.

He was convicted and was sentenced to a second death penalty.

I didn't go to that trial, so I didn't get a chance to meet his wife. When I finally did talk to her on the phone, I didn't take her very seriously. What kind of a woman would fall in love with — and marry — a fellow on death row?

A couple of weeks ago, Smith sent me a copy of some medical records. His wife came to the newspaper to talk about those records.

We talked about the records for a while, and then my curiosity got the best of me. I told her I knew only a little about her. She's a nurse, and she's 12 years older than her husband. She has moved from California to Jefferson City.

Is this an earth-mother kind of a thing? I asked. Or might you be the kind of nurse who seems to fall in love with terminal patients?

No, and no, she said. Furthermore, she said she's not a cause-oriented person. This thing with Smith just sort of happened, she said.

She said she was always very mainstream. She had a normal marriage, raised children, and then the marriage fell apart. Nothing unusual in any of that.

She said her friends back home all thought she was a little bit crazy when she married Smith, but some things you just can't explain.

Well, I guess not.

Now, of course, she is living life on the edge. She says she believes in her husband. That is, she thinks the state has taken advantage of him. He was put on death row for a second-degree murder, she says.

She has already been through several execution dates.

"It's coming down to the wire again," she told me.

If he does get executed, will you be there? I asked.

"I wouldn't want him to die alone," she said.

Then she left. Donna Reed, the woman next door. She said she had to get back to Jefferson City. Something about seeing a lawyer.

JULY 13, 1987

Between a rock and a hard case

7:58, two federal marshals led Jeanne Navies into Judge Stephen Limbaugh's courtroom on the third floor of the federal building in downtown St. Louis.

Navies was in handcuffs. The jury was not yet back in the courtroom after the dinner recess, but the spectators on the defense side, the friends of the defendant, stared at Navies as she was led into the courtroom. She did not return the stares.

Navies was nobody's friend on this particular night. She had been the girlfriend of a man who was a big-time heroin dealer on this city's North Side, and when city narcotics cops busted his house four months ago, she was one of the people arrested at the scene. She had been cooperating with authorities ever since.

The cops, incidentally, seized more than three ounces of heroin that night. The heroin was almost 50 percent pure. The heroin that is sold on the street corners of this city generally checks in at less than 5 percent.

Three ounces of such high-octane heroin is a very big bust in this city, and the city cops offered the case to the U.S. attorney's office, which is how the case got to federal court.

Navies was going to be the government's star witness. She was going to testify that the heroin belonged to her boyfriend. His name is Charles Shurn.

Another potential witness for the government was Charles Taylor. The cops came across him when they traced the utilities at the house they busted and found that the utilities were issued to Taylor. Taylor was a handyman who had done work for Shurn and Shurn's brothers.

Taylor cooperated with the police and even went to court as a potential witness – although he was not called to testify – at a case earlier this month involving one of Shurn's brothers. His name is Larry, and he was convicted.

Navies attended that case with Shurn's family and friends, and she later told cops that she overheard talk about killing Taylor.

Taylor was murdered three days before Charles Shurn's trial. One of Charles' other brothers and another man were caught fleeing from the crime.

The day after the murder, Navies called Jerry Leyshock, the narcotics cop handling the case, and arranged a meeting with him and Debra Herzog, the prosecutor who heads the federal drug task force here. Navies told the two that the gang intended to kill Leyshock, too.

She also turned over to authorities the letters that her boyfriend had sent her from jail, while he was awaiting trial. The letters were incriminating, as Charles told her to testify that the heroin belonged to one of his brothers.

Well, it was easy for a young woman — Navies is 24 — to tell her story on a deserted parking lot — that's where the meeting was held after Taylor's murder — and it was easy for her to repeat her story in the U.S. attorney's office.

But Navies could not muster sufficient courage to tell her story on the witness stand.

After Taylor was murdered, the government had a hearing to revoke the bond of Larry Shurn. Navies was called to the stand and denied having ever told authorities anything.

That's the same tack she tried Friday afternoon at her boyfriend's trial.

"Are you saying that you did not meet with me Tuesday on the parking lot of St. Ambrose?" asked Herzog.

"No, I did not meet with you," said Navies.

"Are you saying you did not give us these letters I have in my hand?" asked Herzog.

"No, I did not give you those letters," said Navies.

"Are you saying you were not in my office this morning, and you did not say, at that time, that the heroin belonged to Charles?" Herzog asked.

It was very unconvincing testimony, especially since Herzog was able to call people who had been present at the meetings and was able to show the jurors the letters that Charles Shurn had written to Navies. Her denials certainly didn't impress the jurors, who convicted Shurn later that night.

After her testimony in the afternoon, she was arrested for perjury, which was why she was in handcuffs when she was brought by the defense as a witness in the evening. She repeated her denials. She was extremely nervous, like a rabbit might be if it were to find itself between a bobcat and a wolf. How does a young woman get herself in such a position?

After her testimony, I asked Leyshock if she was a junkie.

No, I think she just fell in love with the wrong guy, he said.

JUNE 20, 1999

What some men – at any age – will do for love

True love never runs smooth, and that's a thought James Bandy can console himself with as he sits in the St. Louis County Jail and contemplates the future. Or maybe he won't be contemplating the future. The future looks grim. Maybe he'll be thinking about the past.

The past is a love story. A very strange love story. "It started five and a half years ago, when I put a personal ad in your newspaper," Bandy told me when I visited him Friday morning. "I forget the exact words. 'A young 59-year-old widower seeks female companionship.' Something like that."

It was a simple ad. Bandy did not try to depict himself as some kind of big deal, which is fine because he wasn't. Still isn't. He retired on disability in 1985 – he has a bad back – and his total income consists of his monthly $728 disability check. His first marriage had ended in divorce after 13 years. That marriage produced two kids. He hasn't seen them in years. His second marriage lasted 18 years and ended with his wife's death in 1993.

A few months after her death, he put his ad in the paper. It worked. He got a response. In February 1994, he had his first date with Louise. They went to Red Lobster for lunch. A couple of days later, he sent her a dozen red roses for Valentine's Day. He was in love.

She had told him, he says, that she was a 62-year-old widow. She wasn't. She was 66. That wasn't so bad. She was a good-looking 66. The harder truth was that she was married.

She told him these truths a month or so after their first date, when it was becoming clear to her – it had been clear to him from the very first – that the relationship had possibilities. So, yes, she was married, but her husband was in a nursing home with Alzheimer's and he hadn't recognized her in four years, so she didn't feel married. That made sense to Bandy.

"We could work through that," he told me.

The relationship continued. But it was a rocky relationship. Part of the blame has to go to Bandy, he acknowledges. He's a jealous guy. But part of the blame should go to Louise, he thinks. She wasn't always the most stable person around. Incidentally, Louise has an unpublished number. Even working through an intermediary in law enforcement, I have been unable to get in touch with her. Oh, well. She will have her opportunity to discuss this in court.

Bandy and Louise broke up in late 1997, and he moved back to the state of Washington, where he had lived for several years with his late wife. He stayed in touch with Louise, though, and after her husband died in early 1998, Bandy and Louise decided to give their relationship another try.

"I was thrilled," he told me. "I was deeply in love with that woman. Still am."

So he came back here to be with her, but once again, the relationship was rocky. Things would go good, and then things would go bad. Things were at their best in November 1998, when he went to a pawn shop on Telegraph Road and spent more than $400 to buy her a "commitment ring." But a couple of weeks later, she called the police when he waved a knife at her during an argument.

"I had no intention of hurting her," he told me.

Nevertheless, he got locked up, and he did 17 days before Louise decided that she wasn't going to testify against him. He didn't realize it, but life had definitely turned into a country song.

He got out of jail and promptly had another fight with Louise. He decided to put St. Louis in his rearview mirror for good. He hopped into his 1985 Cadillac Eldorado and headed back toward Washington. A man and his car.

He was busted in Montana. A misunderstanding, is the way he describes it. He had already pulled off the road to sleep, and he popped a couple of beers, and a highway patrolman came along and didn't believe he had stopped for the night. Something like that. He had no money to pay the fine, and so he did 57 days.

From jail, he called Louise, and she told him he could come back. He did, and for a couple of wonderful weeks, he was glad he had. Then she gave him the boot again, and he ended up sleeping in his car in Belleville. There was another misunderstanding with the police — this one involved an expired license — and his car was impounded. He began staying at the Salvation Army shelter.

Finally, he got his May check, and he bought his car back from the impound lot. Oh, had he only followed his inclination to head toward the Great Northwest again! Instead, he drove back to Louise's place in Lemay.

She was sitting on her front porch chatting with some guy. Bandy pulled up. He got out of his car. He said things. Then he got back in his car and drove away. A few minutes later, he came back. The guy was gone. Louise was on the porch alone. Seventy-one years old, but still a looker.

"Louise, we've got to talk," Bandy said.

"I've got nothing to say," she said, and she turned and walked into the house.

Bandy went back to his car. He sat there for a moment. Technically, he was a 64-year-old man, but as far as emotional maturity is concerned, do guys ever really get much past 16? Especially when they're in love?

"I should have driven away," he told me.

Instead, he stepped on the gas, achieved ramming speed and smashed into her house. Yahoo. That would show her.

He was arrested and charged with first-degree assault. Louise was not hurt or anything, but she could have been. He was also charged with armed criminal action. That's for using a weapon. The weapon in this case was the 1985 Eldorado.

Now everything is messed up.

"I'm looking at 60 years," Bandy said wistfully. "I've smashed up my car. I'm flat broke. And I'm still in love."

MARCH 20, 2005

Prisoner of love misses demeanor of open romance

Jim Bandy got out of prison last month on his 70th birthday. His only present was from the state — a bus ticket to St. Louis. He called the other day from Dismas House.

"I want to see Louise," he said.

Oh my gosh. We're going to get in trouble again. That's what I thought.

Regular readers might remember Bandy. I first wrote about him in 1999. He was in the St. Louis County jail charged with assault and armed criminal action. It was a strange case in that he had never been in real trouble before. Generally speaking, if a fellow can hit 35 without getting in serious trouble, he's going to be all right. White-collar crime is a different deal, but Bandy was a long way from that. He had gotten in a fight with his girlfriend and he drove over to her place to talk. She said she didn't have anything to say, so he sat in his car for a few minutes and then he decided that he was going to show her. So he drove into the side of her house.

That turned out to be a very poor plan. In the first place, he was charged with a couple of serious felonies. In the second place, he lost his car — a 1985 Eldorado — which was about the only thing he had. In fact, he had been living in it. So he ended up losing all of his possessions, including his ex-wife's ashes, which he had been hauling around.

I treated the matter as a love story gone bad, and I was roundly denounced for romanticizing domestic violence. "McClellan asks, 'As far as emotional maturity is concerned, do guys ever really get much past 16?' The superficiality, ignorance and tacit approval for violence implicit in the question make the mind reel," said one letter to the editor.

Fortunately, I was only denounced. Bandy went to trial, was convicted and sentenced to 12 years in prison. He was 65 when they led him out of that courtroom. I figured he'd been given a life sentence.

So it was nice to hear from him the other day. But he wanted to see Louise? That was the girlfriend whose house he had rammed in 1999. Furthermore, the parole board had made it very clear, he told me, that he was to have no contact with his victim. Let's have coffee, I said.

The next day, we went out for coffee. Bandy's health is not too good. He walks with a cane. He said he has a touch of emphysema, but he still smokes. We ran through the small talk. How was prison? Awful. How did the other fellows treat a 65-year-old rookie? The young guys were very disrespectful.

Then we got to the business at hand. I asked if he had been in touch with Louise when he was in prison. Yes, he said. They had corresponded. Had they seen each other since he'd been out? Yes, he said. You could get in trouble, I said. I've been in love with her since the first day I met her, he said. I'll need to talk to Louise, I said.

The next day, she called. She told me she had written the parole board while Bandy was in prison and had asked that he be allowed to see her, she said. She said she had also called somebody at Dismas House and made the same request. Both times the answer was no.

I asked about her family. I had a vague recollection that her relatives had been among those who had denounced me. Louise said her family did not think she should see Bandy. She said she understood their concerns. After all, he had driven his car into her house. But still, this was her life. She did not like having to sneak around.

Who can blame her? Bandy is 70, and she is a little bit older. Yet here they are, sneaking around like high schoolers. Hiding from the government, hiding from her family. Why can't they be treated like adults?

Besides, Bandy did his time. He made a mistake and he paid for it. He's sorry for what he did. Isn't he? I asked him about it.

"I meant to put a hole in her wall, and I did," he said. But it was the wrong thing to do, wasn't it?

"I wouldn't do it again," he said. "I want to be with Louise. I don't have that much time left."

Maybe I was right five years ago. Maybe this really is a love story.

NOVEMBER 15, 1989

Cabbie and contessa? Don't mensch-tion it

Boaz Rafaeli walked into the courtroom Tuesday morning wearing handcuffs and the gray uniform of a County Jail inmate. He indicated that he wanted to plead innocent to a charge of harassment, so the judge set a trial date for late January.

The trial probably won't be a big-time media event – harassment is a misdemeanor – but there is one media person who ought to attend. That person is Woody Allen. This is his kind of story. It's a story with no heroes, and, if there's much goodness in the story, the people aware of the goodness are not talking.

Incidentally, not all the people who are talking tell the story in the same way. But everybody agrees on certain points.

The starting point, for instance. Everybody agrees the story started 10 years ago.

Ten years ago, Rafaeli was a 27-year-old cabdriver in Jerusalem. He had a wife and two small children.

One day, Lois Gould, a wealthy St. Louis woman, climbed into his cab. She was almost 30 years older than Rafaeli.

Despite the age difference, there was an attraction between the two. Woody Allen could make much of this.

In the next couple of years, Gould returned to Israel twice. The cabdriver and the wealthy widow saw a lot of each other during those visits.

In November of 1981, Rafaeli walked out on his wife and children and came to St. Louis to live with Gould.

"She pulled me out of my marriage," Rafaeli said last week in a jail-house interview.

That, too, is something we'll leave to Woody Allen.

At any rate, Rafaeli came here and lived a fine life. He didn't work.

In April of 1982, Rafaeli and Gould were married.

Gould, incidentally, is the president of the congregation at Temple Emanuel. The temple was the center of the couple's social life.

There are those at the temple who now speak disparagingly of Rafaeli, but — at least on the surface and perhaps out of respect for Gould — the young Israeli initially was welcomed into the fold. He even taught religion to the children.

In the early years of the marriage, the couple projected an image of happiness. They even appeared together on the Sally Jessy Raphael Show to talk about their successful "older woman, younger man" relationship.

But by the summer of 1988, the relationship was in tatters.

Rafaeli went to California and Las Vegas. And when he returned, he was told that he was no longer welcome at his wife's home in Ladue. She filed for divorce.

Rafaeli retained Chester Love, one of the city's top divorce attorneys. Rafaeli had signed a pre-nuptial agreement, but he argued that it should be ruled invalid because he had not understood what he was signing. He requested temporary maintenance while he contested the divorce.

A judge upheld the validity of the pre-nuptial agreement. Love withdrew from the case.

In October 1988, Rafaeli was charged with violating a protective order that prohibited him from going to his wife's home. In January 1989, he was charged with violating a protective order that prohibited him from going to the temple.

Rabbi Joseph Rosenbloom said the congregation had been forced to take action. He said that Rafaeli had become a nuisance, constantly cornering people and trying to talk them into helping him get back together with Gould.

"We would have preferred staying out of it," he said. "But there are other temples he can go to. We wouldn't have abandoned him if he had been a mensch."

Mensch is Yiddish for a "sensible, mature, responsible person."

In the eyes of the law, certainly, Rafaeli was not a mensch.

He was arrested several times for trying to contact his wife. In May, he was convicted of violating a protective order and was sent to the County Jail to await sentencing.

He was released in July and sentenced in October to 60 days on each of five counts.

In addition, he faces additional charges of harassment for allegedly making repeated phone calls to Rosenbloom and for allegedly threatening a temple employee.

Not surprisingly, Rafaeli sees himself as a victim. He thinks the temple sided with his wife because she has money.

"I don't mean to harass anyone," he told me. "I love and adore my wife. I only tried to talk to her and then to talk to my rabbi. Your culture is strange when a man cannot talk to his wife and his rabbi."

Rosenbloom, meanwhile, has offered to give Rafaeli a one-way ticket back to Israel. He has refused the offer.

"What would I tell my family?" he asked me.

It's too bad he can't tell them to see the movie. This is a story for Woody Allen.

JUNE 28, 2013

Recalling Emma's deadly potato soup

Aloys Schneider was a farmer in St. Charles County in the years between the World Wars. Lou Kampman is one of his grandchildren. Kampman wrote me a note after reading Monday's column, which was about a poisoning case in Springfield, Mo.

"Today's column reminds me of my own grandfather's death from arsenic poisoning. He was murdered by his third wife, Emma Hepperman. She was convicted of murdering Mr. Hepperman and attempting to murder his teenage daughter. Prior to these, she poisoned several other people," he wrote.

That was enough to send me to the clips to look up some old stories.

Emma Sarana was born in Steelville in 1894. She married her first husband when she was 14. He was 33. He died 17 years later, allegedly from drinking ice water while overheated. There was no autopsy.

Emma went on to have six more husbands. Most of them died. Suspicions were first raised after the death of her fourth husband, Bert Roberts, and his mother. They died after eating potato soup. The doctor who treated Roberts insisted he had been poisoned. A coroner's jury decided he had died of acute gastritis.

Little is known of the fifth husband.

Schneider was number six. They were married in 1937. Schneider's six kids from his first marriage were already grown. One of those kids was Antoinette Hepperman, Lou's mom. She later told Lou that none of the family trusted Emma.

The newspaper stories confirmed that. Three years after Schneider's death and shortly after Emma was arrested for the poisoning death of her seventh husband, a coroner's jury was called to investigate Schneider's death. One of the witnesses was Alphonse Schneider, the dead man's brother. He told the jury he had lived with his brother and Emma on the farm for a short time, but he left because he couldn't get along with Emma.

Here is the way the newspaper described his testimony: "She told me three times she wanted to kill me," he testified. "One day, in the midst of a quarrel, she said she wanted to cook me some soup." Schneider leaned close to the jury and said, "I sure am glad I didn't eat any of that soup."

But nothing seems to have come of the coroner's jury. Most of the clips deal with the death of Tony Hepperman, Emma's seventh and last husband.

He was 53, a widower who lived on a farm 3 miles west of Wentzville. Three years after Schneider's death, Emma placed an ad in a St. Louis newspaper. It was under Situations Wanted. She gave her name as Emma Lee. Frank Lee had been her second husband. (The newspaper stories noted that his whereabouts were unknown.) Emma listed herself as a "housekeeper for a motherless home; neat and pleasant." Her address was a rooming house on South Vandeventer Avenue.

Hepperman responded to the ad. Emma came out to take a look at the farm. She reportedly said, "I like the place, but what I really want to do is to get married. I don't want to be a housekeeper. I'll tell you what I'll do, I'll work for two weeks. If you like me and want to get married, we'll do that. If you don't like me, I'll go back to St. Louis and you won't owe me a cent."

Hepperman took the deal.

By the way, Emma was 46. She was described in one of the stories as "plump and white-haired."

Her ad ran in March. She married Hepperman in April. He died in May. They had been married six weeks.

One of Hepperman's daughters lived with them. She became very ill, too. She lost 23 pounds in three weeks. She testified that whenever she felt nauseated, Emma would say, "Eat some soup."

Potato soup was Emma's specialty.

Emma was arrested after Tony Hepperman was taken to St. Joseph's Hospital in St. Charles. He told doctors he thought he had been poisoned. After his death, an autopsy confirmed his suspicions.

The trial was moved to Franklin County because of publicity. Emma faced a jury of farmers. That probably did not work to her advantage. Too many of her husbands had been farmers themselves.

A store clerk testified that Emma bought fly paper soaked in arsenic and said she wanted it for water bugs. One of Hepperman's sons said he had visited several times and noticed that Emma never seemed to eat. She always said she wasn't hungry, he testified.

Emma was convicted and sentenced to life in prison. She served 27 years. Her sentence was commuted in May 1968 and she was released without supervision. I was unable to find any notice of her death.

Lou Kampman told me that nobody in his family ever ate potato soup.

DECEMBER 29, 1999

Despite a bungling partner, Mary's marriage thrives

"It was 20 years ago today, Sergeant Pepper taught the band to play."

The morning of December 29, 1979, was overcast in Tucson. Not just a little bit cloudy, either. It looked like rain. Wouldn't you know it? The wedding reception was supposed to be in her parents' back yard, and now it was going to rain. The weather was the last straw. Mary was ready to cry. Maybe she should call the whole thing off.

But, of course, it was too late. Weddings have a momentum of their own. Too many people are involved. Too much work goes into the planning. You can't call a wedding off because of bad weather.

That's true even if you believe in omens, and the omens for this wedding had been ominous from the beginning. Mary was supposed to have gotten her engagement ring at Christmas a year earlier. Her fiance, who couldn't afford much of a diamond, had gotten a break. When his mother learned he was thinking of getting married — at long last, as far as she was concerned — she had given him a diamond stick pin that had once belonged to her uncle. Her son could take the stone and have it set in a ring.

Mary had left town in the fall of 1978 to go to school, and when she came home for Christmas, she thought she was getting a diamond. But there was a problem. (With her fiance, it sometimes seemed there was always a problem.) One of his friends had been busted on some kind of minor drug charge, and the diamond stick pin had been used as bail. It was spending the holidays at Garcia's House of Bonds.

Fortunately, that situation had finally been resolved — the friend got probation and Mary got her ring — and now a year later, the wedding was about to take place. A retired justice of the peace was going to preside.

That, too, was a bit of a problem. He had read the ceremony and balked. He said he didn't mind personalized ceremonies, but this one just seemed wrong. He would earn his money by declaring the couple man and wife at the conclusion of the ceremony, but that would be the extent of his participation.

That was fine. One of Mary's friends had agreed to read the ceremony. It was, by the way, a very standard ceremony, as opposed to a lot of the hippie stuff of that era. Mary's fiance, who considered himself a traditionalist, had added only a single personalized touch, and it came near the very end of the ceremony.

"If anyone knows why this couple should not be joined in holy matrimony, let him speak now or forever hold his peace," Mary's friend read.

It was at that point that the personalized touch kicked in. One of the spectators stood up.

"It's not that I've got anything against marriage," the man said. "It's just that they seemed happy living together, so I just don't see the point in this."

It was just as Mary's fiance had imagined it. The crowd was stunned. There were angry murmurs. How could anybody be so rude?

"Marriage is a sign of commitment," Mary's friend read after a moment, and as she continued, the crowd realized that the rude interloper had been part of the ceremony.

I wish I could tell you that once that realization set in, the crowd appreciated the dramatic moment of which they had been a part. After all, has anybody heard this challenge issued at a wedding without at least a fleeting wish that it be answered?

Sadly, most of the people at Mary's wedding didn't appreciate the drama. Instead, the anger that had been directed at the rude interloper found itself redirected at Mary's fiance, who was standing in front of the crowd, trying vainly not to grin. How could anybody be so silly?

The rain never did come, and despite some lingering bad feelings, the reception was a success. For that matter, the marriage is still rolling along. So much for omens.

APRIL 4, 2010

Miss Mac's turn to make a family

In September 1989, I walked my daughter to her first day of kindergarten. I remember something akin to sadness when the bell rang and Lorna ran into the school. I understood that I had begun to lose her.

Thirteen years later, I helped her move into a dormitory at the University of Illinois. I did fine on the drive to Urbana, but not so well when I started to carry her things up the stairs and into her room. Among the things was a bulletin board with photos of the family — my wife, my son, the dogs and me. Within hours, we would be reduced to photographs. Her life without us was taking shape. I started to cry.

"It's okay, Dad," she said.

"Get hold of yourself," said my wife.

Four years later, I drove with Lorna to northern California. She had joined Teach for America and would be teaching high school biology in Richmond. We drove past the school. It had a rough look. I worried.

A year later, I visited her classroom. She was known as Miss Mac. To my eye, she was hardly older than her students, but she was clearly in charge and seemed comfortable. She was an adult. I was taken by surprise.

Last month, she got married. The ceremony was in the backyard of my wife's youngest sister. My wife and her sister did all the work. My job was to walk Lorna from the house to the garden. I was standing on the patio when she came out of the living room. She looked stunning. Young women in love so often are.

She tilted her head and smiled. "Don't make me cry," she said. I shook my head, as if to say, "Don't worry." I heard one of my wife's sisters say, "Look, he's crying already."

Arm in arm, we walked toward the garden.

Behind us, on the roof of the house, the groom, Darryl Sanchez, had set up a computer so the ceremony could be seen in his native Nicaragua. He has an older brother in Managua. He has friends and family in El Viejo, a small town near Chinandega.

Darryl and his mother, Miriam, came to this country from El Viejo 10 years ago. Darryl's father, Manuel, was already here.

We had dinner at their house a couple of nights before the wedding. Miriam cooked fish. Manuel brought out a bottle of Nicaraguan rum. Manuel likes baseball. He likes baseball so much that he named his second son after New York Mets slugger Darryl Strawberry.

I am a Cub fan and I would have preferred Manuel to have named his second son Ryne Sanchez, or Ernie Sanchez, or even Sammy Sanchez, but as my wife tells me about so many things, "This is not about you."

With the people in El Viejo and Managua watching, I walked Lorna to the garden. Darryl stepped forward. We shook hands and then embraced. Lorna and Darryl then turned toward the young man who was to conduct the ceremony. His name is Rishi Patel. He teaches math at Richmond High. He received his divinity credentials through the Internet. He was holding a book. Inside the book was the ceremony he was to read.

He began reading. I recognized it. It was the ceremony I wrote for my wedding 30 years ago.

I glanced over at my father-in-law to see if he recognized it. He was not enamored of it 30 years ago. That's because I gave the ceremony a dramatic twist. When the preacher said, "If anybody knows why these two should not be joined in Holy Matrimony, let him speak now or forever hold his peace," I had a friend stand up and say, "It's not that I'm against marriage, but these two have been living together and seem happy so I don't see the point."

Our families did not know that was coming, so everybody gasped. But the preacher waited only a second and then talked about the commitment we were making and so on, and people realized the interruption had been part of the ceremony. Still, a lot of people thought it was tacky.

Lorna and Darryl opted for a more traditional approach. The moment came to object, and no one did. I was glad.

The young men and the young women in the wedding party could have come from Central Casting. They were handsome and beautiful and diverse – Latinos, whites, a black, a Jew and, of course, an Indian reading the ceremony. The people watching in Nicaragua probably thought, "The beer commercials are true."

I sat there and I thought, "How did I get here?"

It's a question I have asked myself frequently, and the answer is always the same. My family brought me.

I hope my daughter will be as happy as I've been.

For the love of Bill

MARCH 13, 2006

A bad back is a good stand-in for forgotten midlife crisis

I woke up the other morning and realized it was too late to have a midlife crisis. I had flown past that milestone without giving it any thought. Perhaps there was still time to have a two-thirds life crisis. Certainly, a three-fourths or even a four-fifths life crisis.

But only the midlife crisis is officially recognized. That seems unfair. The latest statistics from the federal government show that a male in this country has a life expectancy of 74.4 years. That means a guy has to have his midlife crisis when he's 37. I'm sorry, but a 37-year-old man is not mature enough to have a midlife crisis. The very least we should require is a bad back, and for most guys, a bad back checks in at about 50.

An aide of Sen. Kit Bond told me that the one thing a veteran politician cannot say as he travels around the state is, "Nice to meet you." That's because he may have met the person before. In fact, for somebody like Bond, who has criss-crossed the state hundreds of times over the years, the likelihood is that he has met most of the people who come to rallies and political dinners. So the proper thing to say is, "Nice to see you." To put a really personal touch on it, if Bond is introduced to a man over 50, he says, "Nice to see you. How's your back?"

"Much better, Senator, and thanks for remembering."

I have been thinking about backs these last few days because mine went out again. That's a great expression. My back went out. Kind of like the rest of my body stayed in and my back went out and tied one on. Hooped and hollered and danced on the tables. Made a fool of itself.

Actually, according to the physical therapist, most of my back stays in. It's one little disc that goes out. Where does it go? A discotheque? At any rate, it slides out of its proper place, and I'm out of commission for a couple of days. I have to spend most of my time lying on my stomach, trying to induce the disc to return to the reservation. By the second day, I can usually walk a bit.

That can be painful, and it's also mentally trying because I have a cat. All cats remember the jungle. They remember the past when they were wild. Dogs don't. They have no memory of their days before domestication. So when I limp around, the dogs pay no attention to me, but the cat watches me for a moment and then stalks me. That bugs me. I'm already in pain. I don't need to be reminded that in a different time, I would now be culled from the herd. But there is the cat, looking at me as if I were prey.

I stamp my foot at the cat. Oh, how that hurts! Normally, that would send her scurrying, but now in my weakened state, I no longer frighten her. She takes a single step back and hisses. My own cat. Terribly misnamed as Daffy, she is a predator, and no spring chicken herself. Fourteen years ago, we bought her at Soulard Farmers Market. Seven bucks.

"We overpaid," I tell her. She hisses again and begins to circle me.

This activity is unusual. That's another thing about staying home. I get to see who does what when we're not around. Mostly, the cat sleeps. The two pugs, on the other hand, take no time off. They post themselves on the windowsill in the living room and bark at everything that goes by.

Lucy confines herself to people and dogs, but Caesar barks at everything. A leaf blows by and Caesar fires away. He barks with the ferocity of a dog who is scared of everything. Snowmen, paper bags and vacuum cleaners are all terrors in his mind. What an imagination he must have. If he were a person, he'd be J.R.R. Tolkien. He has invented his own little world.

I move toward the window to pet him, but the pain is too much and I lie down. Suddenly, the cat is next to me. She purrs. The dogs bark. Bad back or not, I feel pretty good for a guy who is still too young to have a four-fifths crisis.

OCTOBER 19, 2011

A last hurrah for a great sport

Several years ago, when the imminent decline of the newspaper industry was evident even to dullards like me, the local chapter of the Newspaper Guild had its annual dinner at a downtown hotel.

The bar was open, and the free-flowing booze meant that the large crowd was festive. I remember standing at the bar with a friend and gazing at our colleagues in the ballroom. I felt as though I were in a scene from "Gone with the Wind." An era was ending.

"Let's enjoy this," I said to my friend.

I am reminded of that night as St. Louis hosts the World Series. The crowds will be large and festive, and Cardinals fans will be in a celebratory mood, but just beneath the surface of our collective consciousness is the realization that an era is passing.

Baseball was once the national pastime. Literally. Kids got up early on summer mornings and played baseball all day long. They no longer do. Baseball diamonds in our public parks go unused. They are remnants of another time. The next generation of city planners won't include them.

The notion of pickup games is archaic. If kids play baseball at all these days, they play organized baseball. In other words, baseball with adults. That's because adults – fathers, mostly – are trying to pass baseball on to their kids the way their own fathers passed it on to them.

But it isn't taking, and hasn't for a long time.

Why?

Maybe baseball is not frenetic enough for modern life. Kids complain about too much standing around. Outfielders are largely spectators. You only get to hit three or four times a game.

Certainly, the game does not translate well on television. There is too much dead time. Pitchers step off the rubber, batters step out of the batter's box. All for what? A pitch low and outside.

When baseball tries to soup itself up, it only looks silly, like a middle-aged guy wearing his cap backward.

I'm talking about mascots and loud music between innings and induced cheering. I went to a baseball game in Detroit a few years ago. Justin Verlander pitched a no-hitter. When he was pitching in the late innings, electronic messages implored the fans to cheer — as if the situation was not inducement enough.

Football is better suited for television. Networks are not vying for the rights to televise college baseball.

More importantly perhaps, football is better suited for video games. Madden NFL 12 is the rage. There is no La Russa 12 or Herzog 12. Today's video game players are tomorrow's fathers, and when fathers no longer pass the game on to their children, the game is over.

Also, it is more difficult to be a fan than it once was. Some of the blame lies with free agency. Stan Musial was a Cardinal as Ernie Banks was a Cub as Hank Aaron was a Brave. Lineups stayed relatively intact from year to year. Now, today's hero is tomorrow's foe, and something is lost as players move from team to team.

Steroids were another blow. No game reveres numbers like baseball, and no numbers were more sacred than the home run records of Babe Ruth and Roger Maris.

Even casual fans knew Ruth hit 60 — most could name the year in which he did it — and Maris hit 61. (How many people could tell you who scored the most touchdowns in a season?) Mess with the magic at your own peril.

How big a deal did the World Series used to be?

When I was a kid in Chicago, teachers sometimes let us listen to the games on radio. (All World Series games were day games.) Interest was that high, even though Chicago teams were not involved. For a week, we would care deeply about the Dodgers and the Yankees. Imagine that.

Now the games are played at night, and the network worries about ratings. Justifiably, too. According to the Nielsen Co., only 2.9 percent of the nation's homes with televisions tuned in to the National League Championship Series, making it the second-lowest rated NLCS ever. Meanwhile, the American League Championship Series had its lowest ratings ever.

Even here in St. Louis, the ratings for the Cardinals-Brewers series was the second-worst in St. Louis for the team's seven NLCS appearances since 1996.

The trendlines for baseball are not good.

But all that will be forgotten for the next week or so. Fans will be revved up. Tickets will be impossible to come by. The city will be in a good mood.

I'll be thinking about that Guild dinner, and fondly remembering my old colleagues who no longer work here. The world changes, and not always for the better. Nothing we can do about it. In the meantime, let's enjoy this.

DECEMBER 9, 1990

A lawyer and puppy love: Christmas Carol for 1990

In a traditional Christmas story, Dan Bromeier would be a woodcutter. In our contemporary tale, he is an employee of the St. Louis County Parks and Recreation Department.

He is the supervisor at Love Park in Manchester. That's where Bromeier lives. In Love Park. In a house owned by the county. The woodcutter, his wife, Janet, and their three daughters. Jamie is 8. Dawn is 10. Mindy is 13.

In August, Bromeier and his wife took the girls to the Humane Society to pick out a puppy. The girls selected a pup that looked like a cross between a cocker spaniel and a Labrador retriever. They named him Bart.

He was given the run of the house.

On Nov. 12, he wandered away from Love Park.

The little girls were crushed.

The Bromeiers called the Humane Society in case somebody turned Bart in. They called the Animal Control people in the county in case a dogcatcher grabbed him. They put fliers in a grocery store.

Three weeks went by.

The Bromeiers saw a flier advertising a dog. Somebody had found Bart!

Michelle Leszewski is the woman who put up the flier. In a traditional Christmas story, she would be a good Samaritan. That's exactly what she is in our tale.

"We saw him running around, and it was very cold, so we took him in," she said.

She didn't even think about calling the Humane Society. She said she figured that once the Humane Society gets involved, it's a death sentence.

Instead, she put out fliers.

Leszewski couldn't keep the dog, but a family that lived in the neighborhood agreed to keep it temporarily. Eventually, they decided they couldn't keep it, and they gave it to Christopher Kelleher and his wife, Catherine.

In a traditional Christmas story, Kelleher would be a lawyer. That's what he is in our story, too.

Earlier this week, the Bromeiers saw one of the fliers Leszewski had put up.

"You found our dog!" said the woodcutter's wife.

Leszewski was thrilled. As befits a good Samaritan, she had been hoping that the story would end happily. She traced Bart to the Kellehers.

The woodcutter called the lawyer.

The lawyer demanded $93.

He said that's how much he had spent on the dog. Bromeier said he didn't have $93. He and his wife went to the lawyer's condo and tried to plead their case.

"This is our children's dog," they said. "Doesn't that mean anything to you?"

The lawyer, who has no children, said it did not. He had spent $93 on the dog and, furthermore, he liked the dog.

"I suggest you get a new dog. I'm keeping this one," Kelleher said.

At least that's what the Bromeiers say he said.

They then notified the county police department. An officer visited their home in Love Park and promised that he'd try to get the girls' dog back.

The next morning, the woodcutter's wife called me.

I called Leszewski to confirm the story. She confirmed it and added that she was very upset with the Kellehers.

I then called Kelleher at the Clayton law offices of Suelthaus & Kaplan.

When I asked Kelleher about the dog, he said, "At this point in time I don't have any comment." Doesn't it bother you that the dog belongs to three little girls? I asked.

"This isn't about little girls. It's about a dog that didn't have tags," the lawyer said.

Read the paper this weekend, I suggested. The story will be about little girls, their dog and Christmas, I said.

There was a long silence.

"I'd suggest you talk to the Bromeiers tonight before you write anything, "the lawyer said.

That night, the lawyer called the Bromeiers and offered to return their dog. They went to his condo and picked up their dog. Kelleher asked, wistfully it seemed to the Bromeiers, if they would reimburse him the $93 he claimed to have spent. They said no.

Just call McClellan then, and tell him you don't want him to write about this, the lawyer said.

And he gave the family their dog back.

The next morning, Kelleher sent a letter to me via a cab.

In the letter, he claimed it was all a misunderstanding. Money had never been an issue, he said. He had been under the impression the Bromeiers didn't want their dog back.

"After you called me, I talked with the Bromeiers again because they apparently changed their minds and decided that they did want the dog after all," Kelleher wrote.

If I still intended to write a Christmas story, he suggested, at least I have a happy one. He also had advice. Warn people to take care of their pets, the lawyer suggested.

"Unfortunately, not every lost dog like Bart can rely on the kindness of strangers until it can find its way home for Christmas," is the way he ended his letter.

What a happy ending indeed. The little girls and their dog are together again in Love Park.

And I hope that in the future, people will say of Kelleher, as they once said of the changed Ebenezer Scrooge, that "he knew how to keep Christmas well, if any man alive possessed the knowledge."

But this year, if stockings go up under the mantle at the law offices of Suelthaus & Kaplan, Kelleher shouldn't hold his breath.

As Santa once told me, you're only as nice as you are when you think nobody's looking.

APRIL 3, 1994

A life of courage, a message of love

TERRI AND DAVID met at a softball game. She was a waitress. He was in sales.

They dated, and then they got married. That was 10 years ago. David was 30. Terri was 28. The only sad thing about the marriage was the fact that Terri could not get pregnant. So Terri and David decided to adopt. They talked to three agencies and picked up papers from each, but before they sent the papers back, Terri got pregnant.

Cody Armstrong was born in July of 1988.

He was born with pneumonia. Shortly after his birth, the doctors told David and Terri that their newborn son would probably die within two days. David and Terri were devastated.

"It went from being the happiest day of our lives to the saddest," David said.

But Cody surprised the doctors. He survived the first day, and the second, and then he began to get stronger. He spent the first two weeks of his life in the hospital, and then he went home. He was perfectly healthy.

When Cody was 2, David and Terri had another child. Shaylyn Armstrong was born in January of 1991.

Cody loved the role of Big Brother. When Shaylyn would cry, Cody would go over and pat her head. He was always gentle with her.

Otherwise, he was a typical little boy, a rough and tumble kid. Before his third birthday, he was playing tee-ball.

He didn't stay with tee-ball long. Instead, he wanted his father to pitch to him. Day after day in the back yard, David would pitch and Cody would hit.

So it went in the spring and summer of 1992.

One evening in early September, David came home ready to pitch — and Cody said no. He had a headache. He was tired.

David and Terri figured he had a cold.

After Cody continued to feel lethargic for several days — it was so unlike him — David and Terri took him to the doctor.

He's got a sinus problem, the doctor said. Because Cody also seemed dehydrated, the doctor suggested he spend the night in the hospital. After a night hooked up to IVs, Cody felt much better.

But David and Terri were persistent about the headaches. Were the doctors sure there was nothing wrong with Cody?

The hospital did a CAT scan.

David was at work when the results came back, and he drove to the hospital to pick up his wife and son. Cody, who felt so much better, came running down the hall to meet him, but Terri looked stricken.

"Brain tumor," she whispered to her husband. He almost passed out.

Later that month, the doctors operated to remove the tumor.

"I don't want you to get your hopes up," the surgeon told David and Terri. "It looked malignant."

Tests indicated that the surgeon had been right. The tumor was malignant. It was a form of tumor rarely found in children.

But David and Terri never gave up hope. Neither did Cody. The surgery had left him partly paralyzed on his right side. As winter turned into the spring of 1993, he began to regain his strength. Although he still had very limited use of his right arm, he wore a Velcro glove on his right hand so he could still swing his toy bat.

During that winter and early spring, he had seven magnetic resonance imaging tests done on the tumor. The news was good. The tumor seemed inactive.

The eighth test was conducted in April. The tumor was growing.

This time, his parents were prepared. They had been reading medical literature and talking to doctors all over the country. They took their son to Duke University. They were looking for a miracle.

After four days of treatment, the doctors said it was hopeless.

David and Terri and Cody returned to St. Louis.

Cody seemed strong and healthy until June 18, which was David's birthday.

Then his condition worsened. For three days in late June, he seemed to slip in and out of consciousness. On June 27, David and Terri called a visiting nurse to come to their home. He looks bad, they said.

"He's in a coma," she said.

David carried his son into the living room. He sat down in a recliner, and held his boy in his arms. It felt good. For the past few days, Cody had been in pain and uncomfortable and had not wanted to be held.

"It's OK to die, Cody," David told his son. Terri said the same thing. Both had read that children will hold on to life because they don't want to disappoint their parents.

"When you get to heaven," said Terri, "paint me a rainbow in the sky. Then I'll know you're all right."

Cody quit breathing.

The next night, Terri's parents came over for dinner. It was a stormy afternoon. Lightning and thunder cracked in the dark sky. But after dinner, the rain seemed to slacken, and David walked to the window.

A huge rainbow stretched from one horizon to another.

So spectacular was this rainbow that it was the lead item on the 10 o'clock news. One station interviewed an 80-year-old man who said he had never seen such a beautiful rainbow.

You can be sure that in the Armstrong house, the story of Cody's rainbow will be remembered this Easter Sunday.

Incidentally, Terri and David are expecting another child in August. This child will never know Cody, but like the rest of the family, he or she will be reminded of him whenever a rainbow paints the sky.

JANUARY 24, 1996

A light approach to a grave subject

LAST WEEK, on an appropriately dark and dreary night, an unusually large crowd assembled at Krueger's Bar, an establishment in Clayton that generally caters to lawyers, ad guys and similar sub-professionals.

It was draft night for the "Ghoul Pool," which is, perhaps, the greatest annual exhibition of sick humor in the St. Louis area. If your taste runs toward bad, you would have enjoyed it. Each participating team in the Ghoul Pool drafts 10 people, and is awarded points if any of those people die in the coming year. To determine how many points, subtract the person's age from 100. Then multiply that by the round in which the person was drafted.

In other words, no team is going to select George Burns. His death would result in no points. To win the Ghoul Pool, you generally need one surprise success, and you'd like to make that choice in a late round. Last year's winning team had Jerry Garcia.

"Rock stars abuse their bodies," said the lawyer who drafted Garcia last year. Then he took a drag from his cigarette, and a quick gulp of his beer. "I wasn't rooting for Garcia to die. That's not what this is about."

No, it isn't. Almost everybody made that point. It's just that every year, a lot of famous people die. If your taste runs to the dark side, why not try to figure out who they'll be?

And so the Ghoul Poolers gathered last week. Sixteen teams. Habeas Corpses, DOA, Flat-Liners, Hannibals Cannibals, the Coffin Counters, the Grim Reapers and so on. Team members sat at tables, going over their notes, comparing their lists.

Anyone in the public eye is eligible — with one exception. No one can draft Stan

Musial. Even the Ghoul Poolers have standards, minimal though they are. No St. Louisan should profit from the death of Stan the Man.

Finally, the lawyer who serves as commissioner of the Ghoul Pool announced that the draft was about to begin.

He called on Habeas Corpses. Their only recent score was Francois Mitterrand.

"Lady Bird Johnson," said the representative from Habeas Corpses.

A murmur ran through the crowd. This was an unexpected choice. Some names are predictable. Maybe a guy's been ill, or, like Salman Rushdie, under a death sentence. You expect people like that to get drafted.

Incidentally, if a sociologist were to study the lists of draftees, he or she might take note that nobody on death row has ever been drafted. With so many lawyers in their number, the Ghoul Poolers understand that the wheels of justice move slowly.

Rushdie, on the other hand, is drafted every year. This year, he went to the Post-Mortems, who also made a nod toward unhealthy habits and drafted Richard Pryor.

Speaking of unhealthy habits, aging rock stars are popular picks. Last year's winning team, Remains of the Day, has changed its name to Remains of the Grateful Dead, but its strategy has remained the same.

Rock stars Keith Richards and Grace Slick were among its latest selections.

Some selections, however logical, were met by groans and boos.

Other draft choices were met with genuine puzzlement until the drafting team explained its reasoning. For instance, one team drafted Bill "Moose" Skowron, a former New York Yankee.

"He played with Mickey Mantle," explained one of the team members.

In most cases, though, the unhealthy habits were better documented. Boris Yeltsin, known for his drinking, was drafted by DOA last year but was snagged this time by Post-Mortems.

The Crypt Keepers, in what seemed like a reach, took a chance on eating disorders and drafted Princess Di.

The health consequences of a weight problem led Grim Reapers to draft Dom DeLuise.

The selections of Yasser Arafat, Saddam Hussein and Hosni Mubarak indicated that the Middle East is still viewed as unstable. No other politician without a history of poor health was drafted.

The plague of AIDS was recognized, of course. Magic Johnson and Greg Louganis were both drafted.

Mostly, though, old age held sway. Frank Sinatra, Jimmy Stewart, Barry Goldwater, Harry Caray, Gene Autry, Perry Como. On and on went the names. One hundred and sixty in all.

Despite the camaraderie that comes from doing something harmless but truly disgusting, there was, I thought, a barely perceptible feeling of sadness behind the laughter.

For the most part, the older draftees seemed like giants, the younger ones like moral midgets.

That is, of course, the nature of the Ghoul Pool, but still, it was something to think about.

FEBRUARY 17, 2014

A measure of the march of civilization

For Valentine's Day, I wrote about Herb and Zelda Glazer. How they met and how they made a life together. Those stories came from Herb. Zelda has Alzheimer's disease. Herb has other stories, too, many of which he has written down so his grandchildren and great-grandchildren will know something about him and Zelda.

One story in particular fascinated me. When Herb was a young child, his grandfather would come home from work and give Herb a dime and a silver bucket. Herb would take the dime and the bucket to a saloon. He'd stand in line with other kids. When it was his turn, he'd give the bartender the dime, who would fill the bucket with beer and Herb would slowly walk home, trying not to spill any of the beer.

I have heard similar stories before. This was in the days before bottled beer. Kids were often sent to saloons to get beer for their dads or grandfathers.

For some reason, I gave it more thought this time. What would happen today if a father gave his 8-year-old son some money and sent him to the convenience store to get a six-pack?

The clerk would call the police. The child would be sent to an emergency foster home. The father would be arrested. People like me would write about it. How could a responsible parent let an 8-year-old go the store alone, let alone go to a saloon? Social media would be filled with demands that the father go to prison. He probably would.

How far we have advanced.

The day I talked with Herb — who doesn't seem at all damaged from his childhoods trips to the saloon — I visited a fellow who has gotten in trouble via that awful combination of computers and sex. The two do not mix well. But mix they do. Pornography, adult chat rooms and so on are very popular. Unwholesome, but popular. Unknown, of course, in the old days.

That's the thing about computers. They make it easy to do bad things. Guys who would never have had the nerve to buy pornography at a bookstore can access it on a computer. Guys who wouldn't make sexual comments to a real woman can do so to a virtual woman in a chat room.

Technology has not been good for everybody.

After visiting with that fellow, I came back to the newsroom and started thinking about the buckets of beer. Those days seemed so innocent. In fact, the country was scandalized when Clark Gable said, "Frankly, my dear, I don't give a damn." If somebody were to remake "Gone with the Wind" today, Miley Cyrus would probably be Scarlett, and the formal dances at Tara wouldn't be so formal.

What I mean is, society accepts almost anything today — anything except kids going to the saloon to get dad a bucket of beer.

So I mentioned the buckets of beer to Tim O'Neil, our resident historian. That was common, he told me. He said the silver buckets of beer that are sold at some neighborhood festivals — I remember them from Strassenfest — are a form of homage to that great tradition.

Another reporter overheard our conversation, and joined in. This happens often when you work around people who eavesdrop for a living. He told us that he had just read a book about a newsroom in Milwaukee around the turn of the last century. "They used to send a copy boy down to a saloon. He'd have this big pole and all the buckets would be on the pole. He'd get the buckets filled with beer and he'd carry them on the pole back to the newsroom."

Wow.

It's not the idea of having a beer at work that sounds nice as much as the attitude that would allow it. Management must have really trusted employees.

I understand that the good old days weren't always so good. Herb Glazer was born in 1933. That was the heart of the Great Depression. What's more, the world was on the verge of falling apart.

Black kids and white kids would have to go to different saloons in those days, too. Gays were well advised to stay in the closet. There was no safety net. Not even food stamps.

Medicine was primitive compared to today. A doctor carried his entire store of technology in a little black bag. (And it was always a he, too.) A family could lose two or three children to a random virus. Graveyards tell those stories.

So I know that things weren't better in every way. Maybe not even in most ways. But still, I think of a time when a child could safely walk a couple of blocks to a neighborhood saloon, plunk a dime on the counter, get his dad's bucket filled with beer, and then walk home and worry about nothing more than not spilling the beer. Oh, how I miss those times, and I was not even here for them.

FEBRUARY 21, 2014

Am I the only one here with a memory?

Sometimes I feel like I am a character in a science fiction story in which I am the only person in the world with a memory.

Let me give you an example of my memory. I remember in 2004 when the state announced it was decreasing funding for the voluntary desegregation program. School districts in the county were given an opportunity to opt out of the program.

I live in Pleasantville, more formally known as Clayton. There was barely a discussion of opting out of the program. Who in Pleasantville could be against diversity? Even the gentlest critics of the program were considered, at best, cranks, more concerned about dollars than children. The high school students had a walkout to show their support for the program. Some parents contacted me and suggested I write a column about this stirring example of civil disobedience.

I declined. How could it be civil disobedience when the establishment was on the side of the protesters? And the establishment was – from the teachers to the principal to the superintendent, Don Senti.

Fast-forward to the present. My colleagues on the editorial page have likened Clayton and other county school districts to lunchroom bullies for having opposed the Legislature's goofy plan to allow mass transfers of students from unaccredited districts to districts of their choice. The tab would be picked up by the unaccredited districts, which would, of course, then careen into bankruptcy.

Lunchroom bullies? Trying to keep the poor kids out? Doesn't anybody remember 2004?

A few days later, my colleagues on the editorial page came up with a proposal to give the bullies a comeuppance. Abolish the successful districts! Make one giant district out of the entire region. As far as equality goes, that's not a bad idea, especially if you believe that if all schools can't be excellent, none should be. And with one big district, soon none would be.

As a card-carrying liberal, I wish that people acted for altruistic reasons, but sadly, they don't. People who vote for school bonds and generally support school districts do so for mostly selfish reasons. They want their kids to have a good education. They want the higher property values that come with good schools.

If we were to create one big district, support for schools would decline dramatically. That is not even considering the logistical problems. Could any student go anywhere? Of course, that would be true only in theory. Earlier this week, I wrote about a family from Wellston whose car was repossessed. What kind of freedom of choice would a family like that have in one big district?

Maybe we could mandate that all schools in the one big district be excellent. Problem solved. Again, though, I have a memory. I remember something called No Child Left Behind. Had mandating success worked, we wouldn't have failing school districts now. The odd thing about this is that my colleagues who are proposing one big district are actually friends of public schools.

On the other side of the debate are people who want to blow up the entire public school system. Many of these people have the best of intentions. They point out that public schools have been failing poor students for decades. They talk about choice and competition.

Others are more vitriolic. They refer to "government schools," and to these people, government is a pejorative. They want government out of education. In one of the Republican presidential primary debates in 2011, Rick Perry was unable to remember the names of all three federal agencies he wanted to eliminate, but he certainly remembered that one of them was Education. (For the record, he also remembered Commerce, but forgot Energy.)

The point is, even without a memory, he remembered Education. These people don't like teachers unions, either. In fact, they don't like unions, period, and they're not so sure about teachers. Too liberal. Too trusting of science.

Perhaps we should be happy that the debate has begun. At least people are talking about education. It promises to be a major issue in the Missouri Legislature this session — if we ever get past guns, that is. In fact, the Legislature has already moved forward with a plan to nullify federal gun laws.

It's that lack of memory again. The legislators don't remember that General Lee surrendered at Appomattox. The war's over, boys. Your side lost.

Maybe we shouldn't have much confidence in the Legislature. Even with a memory, I can't remember them solving a problem this complicated.

AUGUST 19, 2013

Being as smart as I need to be

All during our mild winter, I kept reminding myself — and anybody else who would listen — that we would pay the piper in the summer. July and August are going to be unbearable, I said over and over.

Of course, we have had a very pleasant summer so far, and now people feel the need to constantly remind me of my dire predictions. When I say people, I pretty much mean my wife. And she reminds me for my own good. It keeps me centered. Otherwise, I might feel like I'm pretty darned smart.

That's because I have a granddaughter who acts as if I'm pretty darned smart. Truth is, I happen to be just smart enough to figure that she's playing me, but if she wants to act like she thinks I'm smart, I am happy to play along.

We went to the zoo on Saturday, which was, of course, a very pleasant day. We looked at animals and ate a lot of sugar. My granddaughter will be 3 in September.

Her name is Evelyn Kathleen Sanchez. She is the result of two great migrations. Her mother's family was part of the Irish immigration at the beginning of the last century, and her father's family was part of the Latino immigration at the beginning of this one. Her dad is from Nicaragua.

She calls him Papa. That is part of her Latino heritage.

When Evie was just beginning to talk, she called me Dada. That's because she heard my daughter calling me dad. Since her dad was Papa, I became Dada.

"I don't want to be Dada," I told my daughter. "I've been Dada, and I enjoyed it immensely, but I am past it."

My daughter is like her mother. She is practical. She said if I didn't want to be Dada, I should pick a name and everybody would start calling me that.

I opted for Coach. So my daughter started calling me Coach, and before long, Evie picked it up. So that's what I am these days — Coach. As in, "Coach, let's get ice cream." To which I might reply, "And maybe a cookie a little later?"

Coach and Evie had a fine time at the zoo. My wife was with us. Her name is Nana. The three of us strolled around the zoo. We looked at the zebras. Nana said that zebras were horses with stripes. Evie asked why they had stripes. Nana shrugged.

"It's an evolutionary thing," I explained. "Stripes make them look thinner. Lions and tigers look at them and think, 'Too skinny. No meat on those things.'"

Evie nodded, but Nana said, "Tigers have stripes, too, Coach."

"With them, it's a fashion thing," I said.

"Gorgeous day for August, isn't it?" said Nana.

"It's like the Wildebeest song," I said. "Que sera, sera. Whatever wildebeest wildebeest. The future's not ours to see. Que sera, sera."

Later, after looking at the wildebeests and a few other animals, we went home. I decided to cut the grass. I had just begun when a neighbor came by, and said, "I believe you're missing a wheel."

Sure enough. I was. I retraced my steps and there was the missing wheel in the backyard. It had apparently fallen off because a bolt had come loose. I couldn't find the bolt. What was I to do? I had already started. I didn't feel like stopping and going to a hardware store. The mower seemed to be working just fine on three wheels. I decided to finish the job.

The silence attracted Nana's attention. She and Evie came out. Nana saw instantly that the mower was missing a wheel. "Why don't you put the wheel back on, Coach?" she asked.

I explained that I couldn't find the bolt. More importantly, I had learned that the mower somehow balanced itself on three wheels. Four were preferable, but not necessary.

"It's like a three-legged dog, " I said. "It looks odd, but it's functional."

I began cutting the grass again. Nana took a picture of me with her cell phone. Well, fine, I thought. The grass doesn't know the mower has only three wheels.

That thought bounced around in my mind for a moment. (Then) I remembered a time I took my family to visit a hog farm in Illinois. I had met the farmer and his wife while doing a story, and they had invited me to return with my wife and kids for dinner. We had a great time and while we were chatting, it suddenly struck me that they probably worked seven days a week. I asked if that were true.

The farmer looked at me like I was a little odd. "The hogs don't know it's Saturday, " he said.

Sometimes I'm not so smart. That's a good thing to remember. I'm glad we've had a pleasant summer.

JULY 29, 2012

Bulging bonuses, skeleton staffs

I was at a party in Chicago this summer and I saw her across the room. I knew the polite thing to do would be to walk over and introduce myself, but I decided against it. When I am uncertain what to do, I usually do nothing.

I have always been that way. Once I was standing in the ocean, water up to my waist, and a small shark swam past. It wasn't Jaws or anything, but it was still a shark. It headed toward a group of people about 30 feet away.

Should I have yelled something? I just stood there. The shark took a left turn and headed toward deeper water. The people never saw it.

She would have shouted a warning. That's my guess. She is a forceful person. If she is ever uncertain what to do, she does something. Again, that's my guess.

I glanced in her direction and saw that she was striding toward me.

"Hello," she said. "Aren't you Bill McClellan?"

I am, I said.

"I'm Mary Junck," she said.

She is the CEO of Lee Enterprises, the company that owns this newspaper. I remember reading about her on a media blog called jimromenesko.com after Lee awarded her a $500,000 bonus in March on the very day the company laid off a number of people in Montana.

Romenesko wrote that he called an editor in Montana to get details about the layoffs, but the editor refused to provide any information. I generally find it unseemly when a newspaper person refuses to provide information, but I was sympathetic toward the editor in this particular situation. He was probably scared. There are more editors than there are jobs for editors.

On the day Junck got her $500,000 bonus, another Lee executive, Carl Schmidt, got $250,000.

I bet that money could have saved all the jobs in Montana.

Then again, this is the buggy whip industry, and perhaps those jobs were doomed. But even so, to announce executive bonuses and layoffs on the same day seems almost cruel.

Junck and I chatted for a few minutes. I told her I had taken the train to Chicago. She said that sounded like fun. Neither of us mentioned the newspaper.

I have written about Junck before, and not warmly. Last September, when Lee announced a round of layoffs at this newspaper, I wrote that while the workers were facing uncertain futures, Junck seemed to be like the banks — too big to fail.

If that sort of thing bothered her, she didn't let on. Not when I wrote it, not at the party.

After a few moments of pleasant chit-chat, Junck excused herself and went off to talk to somebody else. We didn't speak again.

On Wednesday, Lee disclosed in an SEC filing that it has awarded Junck 500,000 shares of company stock, valued at $655,000.

The company's executive compensation committee said stockholders would benefit from linking her compensation to the value of the company's stock.

As a stockholder, I hope so. When Lee bought Pulitzer Inc. in 2005, Lee stock was at $44.55. It closed Friday at $1.26. Junck has been CEO for all that time.

By the way, her $500,000 bonus in March was for steering the company out of bankruptcy.

Maybe that represents progress.

Perhaps this does, too — no layoffs were announced on the day the company announced Junck's new $655,000 bonus.

This time, the company waited a day.

On Thursday, four editors at this newspaper were sacked. One had worked here 31 years. His wife used to work here, too. She was sacked earlier this year.

On Friday, the company announced that nine more people in the newsroom and 10 others elsewhere in the company were laid off.

There is nothing Earth-shattering about any of this. People are getting laid off even in healthy industries. I write about these people often enough to understand how hard it is to land on your feet. Good jobs are scarce.

At the same time the workers are stressed, the big bosses are making more and more.

In fact, it seems there is a certain correlation between layoffs and bonuses. The more people you lay off, the better your bottom line. At least, in the short term. You don't grow a business by getting rid of your workers, but in the short term, it works nicely.

So there is a kind of honesty in pairing the announcements, but still, if I had a chance again to talk to Junck, I'd suggest a little more distance between the announcements.

APRIL 18, 2012

Campus funding 'fix' gets an 'F' in my book

Should universities be financially rewarded for student retention and graduation rates?

Absolutely not, I would say, unless we reward them for poor retention and graduation rates, which is, of course, the opposite of what we intend to do.

According to a story in Tuesday's newspaper, the newest fad in higher education is called "performance funding." Both Missouri and Illinois are buying into it.

The fad is being pushed by the National Conference of State Legislatures. That ought to be enough to scare anybody. Think of Missouri state Sen. Jason Crowell making flatulence noises into his microphone while opponents are trying to talk. Are these the people we want reforming higher education?

The operative theory behind performance funding is that universities are inefficient. They cost too much money for what we're getting. To fix that problem, we will tie funding to performance. Retain more students. Graduate more students and graduate them in four years.

That seems reasonable unless you think about it.

A good university should set its standards high. There ought to be programs to help kids who want and need help, but the essential fact of life should be that if students don't meet the high standards, they will not be retained. They will be booted out.

I say this as a former bootee.

I flunked out of the University of Illinois. I have never held that against the university.

The university had high standards. It was my responsibility to meet those standards, and I was not a responsible young man.

I wish I could say that wine, women and song were my undoing, but it was mostly beer. Beer and cards. I played a lot of euchre.

The university was totally indifferent to my problems. It was called the Big U, and everybody knew the Big U did not care about individuals. That was a life lesson — the world does not make allowances for people.

By the way, that is one of the things you want a university to do — teach life lessons. Most of the stuff I got in trouble for not learning is stuff I probably would not remember if I had learned.

For instance, I have a vague recollection of staring into a microscope to look at a slide of some cell. Whatever I was trying to learn was probably not vital to my future.

But to learn that the universe is indifferent — that is something worth knowing.

If funding is tied to retention rates, students will learn a false lesson. They will "learn" that the world does make allowances for people. Because, of course, for them it will. You get what you pay for, and if you pay for high retention and graduation rates, that is what you will get.

Standards will inevitably go down. We will devalue public education.

A private school can be exclusive by limiting admissions. After all, if you want to be exclusive, you have to exclude. A private school can be exclusive on the front end.

But a state school ought to be more accessible. Kids ought to have the opportunity to attend a state school. That means a state school has to achieve exclusivity by excluding people after they are admitted.

Flunking out of school is not the end of the world. I am not pretending it is pleasant. It was not. But you learn from it and move on.

That is what I did. After a stint in the military, I went to Arizona State University. I didn't drink beer and play cards. I smoked pot and played Monopoly. My friends and I played so much Monopoly that we didn't need a board. We had it memorized. Somebody would be on the imaginary St. James Place and roll a 10 and we'd all yell, "Atlantic Avenue!" At the time, it seemed like an achievement.

What if the university's funding had been tied to graduation rates? What kind of lesson would I have learned if I had been given a diploma? That memorizing a Monopoly board is a good thing?

Instead, I relearned that the universe is an indifferent place. That is worth relearning.

In those days, Arizona State was not quite as indifferent as Illinois, and I didn't flunk out. But I did poorly. Again, it was depressing. My self-esteem suffered.

Maybe I shouldn't play so much Monopoly, I thought. I cut down on Monopoly and studied a little, and my grades improved. Another lesson.

I did not study hard enough to graduate, and I give Arizona State credit for that. You should only get what you deserve.

That lesson will be lost if we start this so-called performance funding. Lowering standards will not fix higher education.

APRIL 22, 2012

Caregiving doesn't have to be one-way

Early in the last century, Tom and Pearl Goodding had a small dairy farm three miles outside of Cairo, Mo. They had two sons, Clay and Clyde.

When the boys were teenagers, the Gooddings had their third and final child, Anna Mae. She was born 95 years ago Monday.

Diabetes ran in the family. Tom died when Anna Mae was 7. That was in 1924, the year after two Canadian scientists won a Nobel Prize for the discovery of insulin but before the drug became widely available. Clay died from his diabetes a short time later. So did Tom's sister, Cynthia, who lived on the farm next door.

Pearl married her brother-in-law, Cynthia's widower, and the two farms and families merged.

These were religious people, and Anna Mae remembers going to a Baptist church every Sunday in a horse-drawn surrey.

The Great Depression meant they couldn't sell anything. Not even eggs for a penny. On the other hand, they were a farm family and they never went hungry. Pearl was fond of saying, "Eat it up. Wear it out. Make it do, or do without."

Depression or not, Anna Mae went to high school. She earned a scholarship to the junior college in Moberly, and then another to Northeast Missouri State Teachers College in Kirksville. She graduated and returned home to teach at a one-room school near Cairo.

While at Moberly, she had met a young man, Beuford Powers. He was a redhead like her. Friends teased that they were siblings. He moved to Kansas to manage a paint store. She visited.

They were married in December 1940. Anna Mae was 23.

Beuford was drafted during the war. He served in the Army Air Forces in the Philippines.

After the war, they moved around as Beuford managed paint stores. From Missouri to Arkansas to Oklahoma to Kansas and finally to St. Louis, where Beuford ran a paint store on Cherokee Street.

They had four children – Jeff, Susann, Louann and Scott. Anna Mae sold real estate. She remained religious, but she switched from Baptist to Methodist and finally to Assembly of God.

She often saw the hand of God where others might miss it.

One day in 1987, Beuford wanted to visit a fabric store. He and Anna Mae arrived at the store and saw two members of their church outside. "I don't know why I'm here," said the woman. "I don't sew."

The four of them went into the store. Beuford fell to the floor, dead from a heart attack.

"Those two friends were my angels," Anna Mae told me last week. "He knew I needed somebody right then."

She continued to sell real estate. She was active in her church and volunteered at the Feed My People thrift store. She moved into an assisted living apartment, and then, in December 2011, she collapsed.

She had congestive heart failure. She was nearing the end. As a Christian, she did not fear it. She moved into the Affton home of her daughter, Susann.

Susann wanted help caring for her mother. Through a friend, she heard of Donna Rick, who worked as a caregiver. Donna began caring for Anna Mae on Jan. 10. She was cheerful and hardworking.

But underneath the cheerful surface, Donna's life was a mess. She has a rocky marital history. She has eight kids, four of whom still live at home. Her finances were a wreck. Her credit score was low. She was taking medicine for depression.

She took the job caring for Anna Mae with the understanding it would not be a long-term gig. Maybe it would last a couple of weeks.

When you sit at someone's bedside for hours, you spend a lot of time talking and listening. Donna heard the stories of Anna Mae's life, and she told Anna Mae about her own.

Anna Mae began giving her advice. Soon Donna and her children were attending Anna Mae's Grace Union Church. When Donna got her tax refund, Anna Mae told her to buy a CD and then borrow money from the bank that held the CD. Donna's credit rating has soared.

Anna Mae advised her on real estate, too, and this week, Donna closed on a house in Herrin, Ill.

Anna Mae gave her personal advice, too.

"She's changed my life," Donna told me. "I should be paying her to take care of me."

I stopped by Friday. Anna Mae was sleeping. She seemed to be slipping away. Time is short, but everybody agrees that is fine with Anna Mae, who believes in a life after this one.

In fact, maybe she has hung on this long only in order to help Donna. After all, she has always believed in angels.

FEBRUARY 26, 2014

Caught behind enemy lines, unable to speak Hardware

The sliding glass door in the shower came off its runner, if that is right term for the black thingamajig that attaches to the bottom of the door. This was apparently caused because the clasp – a silver thingamajig – at the top of the door came loose. Actually, it did more than come loose. It fell from its perch, and the sliding door no longer slid. It was stuck in place.

I did not see this as a major issue. It was still possible to wiggle into and out of the shower. Admittedly, the fact that the door would not close meant that water was likely to splash on to the floor, but that did not seem like a big deal, either. The floor is tile.

My wife does not share my equanimity. "Oh, no," she said, as if something awful had occurred. "When did this happen?"

Perhaps it was my imagination, but there seemed to be a note of reproach in her voice. Obviously, the door had been sliding just fine when she had taken a shower earlier.

"It's not a problem," I said. "You can still get in and out."

But to her it was a problem, and it had to be fixed. She picked up the silver thing and looked at it closely. "Get me a Phillips screwdriver," she said.

I felt a jolt of pride that I knew what a Phillips screwdriver was, and more to the point, my wife knew that I knew. Years ago, when I was about to head off to college, my dad, who was an electrician, got me a job as an electrician's helper. I worked on a crew installing streetlights along Lake Shore Drive in Chicago. It was glamorous work, grown-up work.

But the electricians quickly realized that I was totally inept, completely unlike my father, a man they all knew and respected. They also knew I was about to head off to college, so they probably figured it didn't matter that I was inept, as long as I didn't end up in medical school. None of them would have wanted me operating on them.

They teased me. "Hey, Bill, get me the left-handed pliers." It would take me a minute to realize there was no such thing. On and on it went. They'd make up names for tools and I'd look through the tool box trying to figure out what it was they wanted.

So, yes, I took some pride in knowing what a Phillips screwdriver was. I went and got one. My wife did her best to get the clasp back on the glass door, but the clasp kept coming off.

"I'm going to need a new clasp," she said. "Are you going to have time to go to a hardware store today?"

"I'll make time," I said.

She nodded, but didn't say anything. It has long been suspected in our house that I don't really do much.

I go to work every day like a normal person, and I even make and get phone calls at night sometimes, but it has always been assumed that if there are errands that need to be done during the day, I'm the person to do them.

I did, in fact, squeeze a trip to the hardware store into my schedule. I showed a worker the silver clasp.

"This came off a sliding glass door," I said. "I thought I could fix the darned thing, but as much as I tighten it, it keeps coming off." The man took the clasp and seemed to study it. "I used a Phillips screwdriver, " I said.

I am sometimes accused of daydreaming, but I felt like an American soldier operating behind enemy lines. I'm thinking of one of those World War II movies in which Americans put on German uniforms and go behind enemy lines to do commando-type stuff. There is always a scene in which a real German officer is talking to one of the Americans who doesn't speak German so well. The officer seems to suspect something!

As regular readers know, I long ago realized that I have Neanderthal genes. We all do — we know that now — but I am convinced that some of us are more Neanderthalish than others. I can't explain how it happens, but now and then, the Neanderthal genes become dominant.

There was an article in Psychology Today this month by Frederick Coolidge and Thomas Wynn. They wrote that Neanderthals were not innovators. They didn't invent tools. "They appear to have been pragmatists. They did what worked for a very long time until Homo sapiens arrived, and then they went extinct."

Except, of course, we didn't. We walk among you. We still don't understand tools. Why wouldn't there be left-handed pliers? We're pragmatic enough to be content to maneuver around a broken sliding glass door.

The hardware store worker looked at me. I half-expected him to say something in German. Instead, he shrugged. "We don't have any of these, " he said.

I nodded and made my escape. The next day, my wife hired a Homo sapien to fix the sliding glass door.

DECEMBER 22, 2013

Christmas kindness keeps rolling on

Jere Tyrer and Dale Oberkramer are blind. Both lost their sight suddenly. Oberkramer was 43 when a wall and beam collapsed on him nine years ago. Tyrer was injured four years ago when he was crawling under a car to unhook a tow cable and the car rolled over him. He was 52.

Both men were divorced. It has to be especially hard to be alone when you are suddenly sightless.

By the time of Tyrer's accident, Oberkramer had already learned to navigate in the dark world. He was the director of the Lutheran Blind Ministry group at St. Mark's Lutheran church in Eureka. By the way, the church sponsors the group, but the group is open to anybody who is blind. Tyrer joined, and soon he and Oberkramer were close.

Last summer, Tyrer came up with an idea. Why not help somebody at the holidays? Oberkramer liked the plan. Part of being blind is always needing other people's help, especially when you live in an area without public transportation. Turning the tables and helping somebody else sounded cool.

I wrote about their efforts last Christmas. It was surprisingly difficult for them to find a family to help. Most social service agencies were worried about confidentiality and were reluctant to put the men in touch with a family. Finally, a caseworker agreed to help. She gave Oberkramer's number to a mother in Franklin County, who then called Oberkramer with her children's wish lists.

Oberkramer scribbled the items down. "I'm sure it wasn't a pretty sight, " he said. The men had agreed to spend $100 each. That represented three months of scrimping. Two of Tyrer's sisters took them to the Kmart store in High Ridge. The kids' wishes had been simple — clothes and teddy bears and fuzzy boots. With the help of the sisters, the men found everything. The total cost was $207, almost within budget.

Their story appeared on Christmas last year. One reader was touched by the men's generosity and spirit. This person sent each of the men $100. Another person sent $25.

The two men decided to put those donations into a fund to help somebody this holiday season. Other members of the Blind Ministry group got caught up in the spirit. Members would pitch in a few bucks at meetings. Their numbers ebb and flow a bit, but if everybody makes it to a meeting, there might be 10 people.

Bob Wardenburg, who helps coordinate the program for the church, said the effort was really positive.

"It was amazing to see the turnaround. It was like a decision to look outward rather than inward, " he said.

Several months ago, a woman who lives in a town west of St. Louis happened to see an article in a local paper about the group. She called Oberkramer. She explained that she and her husband had young twins who were visually impaired. She wondered if Oberkramer knew of any places where she could get help. He certainly did.

Although the group doesn't have anything for kids, the members are plugged into various agencies. They helped the family get plugged into that network.

"It was great to talk to him, " the mother said. "I have a lot of things to learn as a mom, and it's hard to do it without help. Dale said he could relate to that. I mentioned one of the medical procedures my son was going through, and Dale had been through it himself. These guys just immediately understood what I was going through with my two."

The group also helped in other ways. The father works two jobs, and the family is financially stretched. So the group bought some necessities. For instance, diapers. Also, the group felt it had found a family to help for the holidays. In addition to the twins, the family has a 4-year-old. Oberkramer called the mom and broached the idea.

"He asked if it would be all right, " the mother recalled. "I said it would be wonderful. We have lot of medical bills. It was like music to my ears. I was blown away."

And so the young parents were able to tell their kids to prepare lists for Santa.

Once again, the lists were not extravagant. Coloring books, toys, puzzles. The puzzles are wood and a little blocky. The twins have to be able to feel the shapes. Also, stuffed animals. A Batman cave. Normal kids' stuff.

"Jere came up with another idea, " Oberkramer said. "We're getting food so they can have a big Christmas dinner."

The joy of giving. That's something Dale Oberkramer, Jere Tyrer and their friends understand. And they want the people who sent them money last year to know that those gifts were well used this year. The Santas paid the kindness forward.

AUGUST 26, 2011

Destiny pays visit to buddies in battle

In January 1943, Tom Glancy arrived in Australia as part of the 1st Marine Division. He put his gear in a tent and settled down. A few minutes later, another Marine stuck his head in the tent.

"Any empty beds in here?"

There were. The newcomer's name was Jack Brady. The two young men started talking. Glancy asked Brady where he was from. St. Louis, said Brady. Where'd you go to high school? asked Glancy. Southside Catholic, said Brady. Never heard of it, teased Glancy, who was a CBC grad.

Glancy was 19. Brady was 18. They were both assigned to the 3rd Battalion of the 11th Regiment. Glancy was a forward observer who would call in targets for the artillery. Brady was an artilleryman.

They went to Melbourne together on liberties. They were tent-mates for almost a year.

In December, they participated in the invasion of Cape Gloucester.

They were tent-mates again when their unit regrouped after the fight.

They were part of the invasion force at Peleliu. They were tent-mates again after that very bloody battle.

Then they were part of the force that invaded Okinawa. When that island was secured, they were tent-mates again as they awaited orders to invade Japan.

When the two atomic bombs precluded the need for that invasion and the war ended, Brady and Glancy were sent to China for 90 days. Then they were on the same troop ship back to the States.

They rode together from the West Coast to Chicago on a train, and then to Union

Station in St. Louis. They stood together on the platform and gazed at the crowd.

Glancy saw his family and hurried off to meet them. When he looked back, Brady was gone.

The two men got on with their lives. They put the war behind them. They did not stay in touch. They both went to St. Louis University, but neither knew the other was there.

Brady graduated with a degree in business. He married a girl he had met at the Rail Fence, a hamburger joint on South Grand. He went to work as a salesman at Porter Paint Co. He became a district manager and then a regional manager. He and his wife had five children.

Glancy left the university shortly before he would have graduated. He got a job as a salesman with a steel company. Then he became a liquor salesman. He married a girl from Indiana. They lived for a couple of years in Chicago and then moved to Dallas. They had two children.

Glancy's wife died in 1994. A year after her death, Glancy heard from his high school girlfriend, Beth. She had gone to Visitation. She was a widow and had heard through mutual friends that Glancy's wife had died. He came to St. Louis for a wedding, and the two got together. They married.

In 2006, Glancy and Beth moved into an apartment on the Cardinal Carberry campus in Shrewsbury. Their apartment was in a complex run by Cardinal Ritter Senior Services.

Two years later, Brady moved into the same building. His wife had died in 1999, and Brady's health had begun to deteriorate to the point that his kids thought he should no longer live alone.

The former tent-mates did not know they were living in the same building.

Brady fell and broke his hip and went into the building on campus for rehabilitation. He returned to his apartment and then last year, fell and broke his hip again.

Shortly before that second injury, Beth had a stroke. She went to the rehab building.

Glancy was visiting Beth when he heard a nurse tell another nurse that Jack Brady had fallen again.

Jack Brady?

Glancy went back to his room and got a photo he keeps on his desk. Two young Marines pose for the camera in Australia. They look like kids.

He took the photo and went to the rehab building. He saw his old tent-mate sitting at a table in the cafeteria. When he approached the table, Brady thought, "I think I should know that guy, but I don't."

Glancy put the photo on the table. "Recognize these guys?" he asked.

Beth died last June. Glancy still lives in the independent-living building. Brady lives nearby in an assisted-living building. Glancy visits every Tuesday. They go out to dinner once a month. This Saturday night, they will be at Lester's.

I visited them when they met Tuesday. I asked why they get together only once a week.

"I can't stand him. That's why," said Glancy.

Brady laughed and Glancy joined in.

For a moment, they were young again.

MAY 5, 2012

Don't upset life's delicate balance

My mother foretold her own death. She saw it in a dream. She told my wife, but not me. My mother understood my limitations.

Among them is not having the gift of magic. But because I grew up with a mother who had the gift, I have always believed in it without understanding it. That is to say, I am superstitious.

I was in Forest Park on Tuesday morning with my dogs. As we often do, we were hiking in Kennedy Forest near the zoo.

The sky was dark. Then the rain came. A downpour. I heard the rumble of thunder.

I have been in storms before. I know enough to be wary of tall trees. Sometimes lightning hits a tree and then zaps out to hit a person nearby. A subsidiary strike, it is called. Also, a lightning strike can set up an electrical field on the ground near the tree.

Experts will tell you the best thing to do is to crouch down in an open field, but I have never done that and I have never even seen anyone do it.

What I do is seek shelter under a short tree. That might be the second-smartest or second-dumbest thing to do, but it has always worked for me.

So the dogs and I found a suitable tree to wait out the downpour.

Suddenly, I remembered something. A couple of weeks ago, right after the hoopla about the $656 million lottery jackpot, a couple of friends and I were sitting in my dining room talking about how we would handle winning that kind of money.

The conversation was similar — probably identical — to millions of conversations going on in homes all across the country. What would you do with all that money?

We would be generous, my friends and I assured each other. We'd give money to friends and relatives. Lots of money. Let's say you cleared $400 million after taxes. What's the difference between having $400 million or $300 million?

There is a difference between having no money or some money, and there is a difference between having $1 million or $5 million, but there isn't much difference between having $300 million or $400 million.

In other words, you could give $100 million away without feeling it.

To put it another way, you could give $100,000 each to 1,000 people.

After several minutes of this sort of talk, I announced I was going to the grocery store to buy some beer.

What I actually bought were three Powerball tickets. I thought of that as I stood under the short tree.

I make it a rule not to buy lottery tickets. I like to say, "We're not the kind of people who would win the lottery. On the other hand, we're not going to be hit by lightning."

That is the attitude of a person who is satisfied with his lot. I have been fortunate in so many ways. If life were a game of chance, I'd be holding my chips, folding my hand.

Much of that has to do with age, I'm sure. The young feel invincible. They're risk-takers. As you get older, you shudder to think of some of the things you did when you were young. Mostly, you fear that your own kids will be as reckless as you were.

Maybe it's not wisdom that comes with age. Maybe it's fear.

Whatever it is, I feel like I have made accommodations with the universe. I will not try to win the lottery as long as the universe keeps the lightning away.

For my part, I don't push my luck. I stay away from tall trees during storms. But I don't have to crouch in an open field. I can seek the shelter of a small tree. I don't have to be the smartest guy as long as I am not the dumbest guy. The middle is fine.

The key is to not upset the delicate balance.

I suspect my mother would understand my thinking. Of course, magic is more sophisticated than superstition. They're aligned only in the sense that both acknowledge that there is more to the world than the skeptics imagine.

So the dogs and I stood under the short tree, and I wondered what had possessed me to buy those lottery tickets. A joke. That's all it was.

The thought occurred to me that maybe I ought to go to an open field and crouch down. Maybe getting soaked would serve as some sort of penance.

But I didn't. That's another thing I like to say: "When you're not sure what to do, maybe you shouldn't do anything."

In a few minutes, the rain let up. The lightning never did come. The dogs and I continued our walk. As I sometimes do, I thought about my mother. Perhaps at those times she is with me. You never know. At least I don't. I've never had that gift.

MARCH 26, 2014

Economy on auto-pilot raises scary questions

A friend recently sent me a story from Bloomberg News. Within a couple of decades, technology will eliminate approximately 40 percent of our jobs, the story said.

One of the jobs mentioned was bank loan officer. Give a computer a person's financial history, and it can make a more reliable loan decision than can a person.

I read the story and deleted it. I didn't think about it again until I was driving to work Tuesday morning and heard Debbie Monterrey on KMOX talking about a phone app that will allow a person to learn all about homes for sale in a given neighborhood. Apparently, you can even "tour" the homes with the app.

In other words, you don't need a real estate agent.

That made me think about the Bloomberg story. It will soon be possible to buy a house without dealing with a person. See the house with an app and get your loan from a computer.

When I got to the newspaper, I asked one of the research assistants in our library to help me find the Bloomberg story.

I'm being facetious. We don't have research assistants at the buggy whip factory anymore. Those jobs are long gone. I had to try to find the story myself. I "Googled" Bloomberg and job loss and came up with a number of depressing stories. Unicrest plans 8,500 job cuts. Qantas to slash 5,000 jobs. Barclays cuts up to 12,000. But nothing about the particular story I wanted.

Oh, well. You get the general idea. The economy is shedding jobs. The so-called new economy will have even fewer jobs.

Actually, that's been clear for a while. Last year, a Wall Street Journal story predicted the end of truck drivers. At the moment, there are 5.7 million of them. The story said that within 20 years, trucks will drive themselves. The writer cited the increased productivity of driverless trucks but then gave a nod to the human cost. "It's hard not to feel a swell of fear for those 5.7 million people, a last bastion of decent blue-collar pay."

A swell of fear, indeed.

Of course, people will build and maintain the computers that drive the trucks. Our workers will have to compete with workers all over the world for those jobs. So don't expect big salaries.

In general, the new economy will require fewer workers, but technology will allow them to be much more productive.

I've already mentioned the demise of bank loan officers. What about other bank workers? Earlier this month, Lisa Brown, who covers banking for this newspaper, wrote about the introduction of tablets at PNC banks. The tablets handle transactions. No more tellers.

Why not banks? Gas stations used to have people who pumped gas. Now you pump your own. Grocery stores are going self-service. You check yourself out. You bag your own groceries.

Maybe the most interesting thing about Lisa's story was the online reaction to it. A couple of readers bemoaned the demise of customer service and the loss of jobs. One reader made fun of people who are afraid of innovation. Another simply wrote, "I haven't walked into a bank in at least five years."

That reader is the future. Automatic deposits. Online banking. Even without tablets, brick and mortar banks are facing extinction. For that matter, brick and mortar stores are in trouble, too.

At the moment, the stories about this new economy talk in terms of 10 or 20 years. That is not far off, but more to the point, these things have a way of accelerating. Once the rock starts rolling downhill, its speed increases.

We are already past the days when a person with a willingness to work could find a job and support a family. Our fathers and grandfathers didn't need an education. Just a willingness to work. Maybe a strong back. The jobs they once held are gone.

We have now reached the point where a college degree no longer comes with a guaranteed ticket to the middle class.

High unemployment is coming. The new economy won't be able to use us all. Yet higher productivity could mean no reduction in goods.

What will a largely jobless economy look like? What becomes of the truck drivers and the tellers and the loan officers and the construction workers who used to build brick and mortar stores? Who will be able to buy the houses that can be found without a real estate agent? Who will impress the computer enough to get a loan?

How will we provide for everybody? Will we share jobs? Will all citizens get an annual stipend?

Nobody in politics talks about any of this, but it's coming.

FEBRUARY 19, 2014

Families at the heart of school transfers

Racquel Wooten wants her kids to get a good education. That hardly seems newsworthy, but Racquel and the kids live in a duplex in Wellston, so they find themselves involved in one of our region's biggest and most complicated news stories.

They're in the Normandy School District, which lost its accreditation in 2012. State law says that kids in an unaccredited district can transfer to an accredited district, with costs being borne by their home district. After legal challenges to that law failed, kids from Normandy and Riverview Gardens, another unaccredited district, were allowed to transfer at the start of this school year.

Racquel's five children transferred to the Brentwood School District.

Actually, this was not the first disruption in their schooling. They used to go to Wellston schools, but the state dissolved that district in 2010, and the Wellston students found a refuge, of sorts, at Normandy.

By the way, that was not a big story. Cynics might point out that almost all the students involved were poor, and news follows its readers, which tend to be middle class.

The failures of the Normandy and Riverview Gardens districts were not confined to the poor. Students could transfer to any district within their county or in an adjoining county. According to the letter of the law, the home districts would be responsible for all costs, including transportation, but that would have quickly bankrupted Normandy and Riverview Gardens, something the poorly conceived law did not take into account.

So the educational establishment reached a compromise. The unaccredited districts would be required to provide limited transportation options. Riverview is providing transportation to Mehlville and Kirkwood schools. Normandy chose Francis Howell.

But if parents were willing to provide transportation, they could send their kids anywhere. Or, they could stay in the Normandy or Riverview Gardens schools.

There was much discussion at the duplex in Wellston.

Britney, 17, and Brian, 15, are the oldest of the five kids. Britney was a straight-A student at Normandy. She was ready to start her junior year. She wasn't keen on another disruption. She remembered her sense that the Normandy teachers looked down on the Wellston kids who had transferred in. She didn't want to go through that again.

Brian wasn't such a hot student, but had played JV football as a freshman. He was about to start his sophomore year. He was more open to transferring.

The three youngest kids, Chineye, 10, Canaan, 9, and Raven, 7, were pretty much neutral. Except for Canaan. He didn't want to transfer.

But the father of the three youngest, Clarence Jones, liked the idea of getting them out of Normandy schools. So did Racquel. And she favored a clean break. She didn't want to send the kids to Francis Howell with the other Normandy kids. She wanted them to make new friends and be in a new environment. She researched other districts. She finally settled on Brentwood.

All five enrolled for the fall semester. Britney and Brian felt a little behind academically. But Brentwood provided resource classes and counselors — and perhaps most importantly, the two felt welcomed. Britney took regular classes instead of the honors classes she had routinely taken at Normandy High, and she ended the semester with all A's and B's. She was also a cheerleader.

Brian had a B average and started on the football team.

The younger kids did fine, too. Even Canaan came around. His new school had a playground.

So everybody was happy with the decision to transfer.

Last month, the family car, a 12-year-old GMC Yukon, was repossessed. Suddenly, transportation was gone. Racquel is a cook at a Red Lobster. She gets about 25 hours a week. Clarence is a self-employed plumber, but work is hard to find. The family's credit is not good.

So how do the kids get to school? "With the grace of God, " said Clarence. More literally, it's through the generosity of friends and family. Racquel is forever trying to set things up. But when you are dependent on other people's schedules, things are uncertain. Often, now, the kids are late.

Public transportation is an option, but not a good one. Britney said the trip requires either four buses, or two buses and MetroLink, with a transfer on the Metro.

The family gets some help. Brian is on the wrestling team, and the coach gives him a ride home from practice and meets.

Still, it's a struggle. All the kids want to stay at Brentwood, but it's hard to figure out how the logistics will work. Just as it's hard to figure out the big story itself, except that at the heart of it are people like Racquel, who simply want their kids to get a good education.

NOVEMBER 8, 2013

Family with broken past creates happier present

Herb was a handsome young man with dark, wavy hair. He was from Belleville. Laura was from St. Louis. They met at a factory in St. Louis where both were working in the early days of World War II. The factory must have been involved in the war effort because Herb's work got him a deferment.

They became a couple. They were married Dec. 31, 1942.

Their first child was born in November 1943. The next in December 1944. Their third in '46. Their fourth in '47. And so on until their ninth child was born in June 1953.

But this was not the Brady Bunch. No happy, funny sitcom here.

Herb had a hard time keeping a job. He liked taverns. He was sociable. Shortly after their second child was born, Laura moved in with her mother. She accused Herb of having a girlfriend. The separation was short-lived. They were soon back together. More babies followed. After the fifth child was born, they lost their apartment and moved in with Herb's parents.

It was a small house. When Herb lost another job, his father called authorities. Herb was sentenced to six months in the county jail for nonsupport.

While he was in jail, baby No. 6 was born. About that time, baby No. 5 contracted polio.

Herb got out of jail, and nothing changed. Baby No. 7 came along. Shortly after baby No. 8 was born in 1952, Herb was sentenced to another six months.

In October of 1953, four months after baby No. 9 was born, Herb was sentenced to a year in prison for nonsupport. According to family lore, the judge had lost patience with both Herb and Laura, and told Laura that she could have her children or her husband, but not both. This had to stop. She chose her husband.

In a letter to one of her children years later, she wrote, "The vows are for better, for worse, in sickness and health, till death do us part." She wrote that she had always loved her kids.

At any rate, they were taken away. Days later, Laura returned to court and pleaded for her children. The judge gave her the three oldest, all boys, but said the rest would be put up for adoption. Daughters four and five were adopted by relatives. Daughter six was adopted by Herb's father's boss. Seven and eight — a boy and a girl — were adopted together by strangers. The ninth child, a boy, was also adopted by strangers. The three last were too young to have real memories of their life as a large family.

Herb got out of prison but became ill. He was diagnosed with tuberculosis. After a lengthy illness, he died in 1965.

As the children grew into adults, Nos. 1, 2 and 3 had sporadic contact with Nos. 4 and 5, but the others had separate, and happy, lives.

The sixth child, Donna, graduated from Cleveland High School in 1967 and went to work at Ralston Purina. She married a co-worker. They had two sons, born in 1973 and 1977.

Donna had never made any effort to contact her birth family. But she wondered about medical history. She looked in the Belleville phone book. Laura was listed. Donna sent her a note. Laura called. Could she come over? Yes, said Donna. Through Laura, Donna made contact with two of her older brothers, but not much came of that. Also, Laura gave Donna the address of one of the girls who had been adopted by a relative.

Laura wanted to establish a relationship, but Donna balked. That was in 1979.

In 1982, Laura called again. "I need a favor, " she said. "I need one of your kidneys." No, said Donna. She explained that she had two children of her own. Laura died later that year.

Like I said, hardly a sitcom.

But things were beginning to move. Donna and her sister were writing back and forth. Contact with the three older brothers was sporadic, but existed.

This summer, those five got together. It went well. They wondered about finding Nos. 7, 8 and 9. (The sister who had contracted polio as a child was in an assisted living facility.)

Donna put herself in charge of the search. She quickly learned there is a lot of help available. Search angels, they are called. She found seven, eight and nine.

She contacted them by Facebook. After some hesitation, Nos. 7 and 8 agreed to get together with their long-lost siblings. No. 9 declined.

The rest of them met on Labor Day. Donna said it was remarkable. They liked each other. Everybody seems normal. They're middle-class people and retired, approaching retirement or thinking about retirement.

They're planning an even bigger get-together the Saturday after Thanksgiving. Aunts, uncles and cousins will be there. Kids, too, of course. Why not? It's a family thing.

JUNE 16, 2013

Father's letter was 'more than words'

William Hill was born in Sikeston in 1932. He was soon joined by seven younger siblings. When he finished sixth grade, he quit school to help support the family. He got a job in a junkyard.

Truth is, he did not miss school. He was cross-eyed, and consequently the target of bullies. Perhaps the condition could have been treated surgically, something his family could not afford.

Dottie was born in Sikeston in 1934. Her parents worked at the International Shoe factory. Then her dad got a job with a shoe repair company and the family moved to Iowa. When she was 15, her family returned to Sikeston to visit relatives. One of her cousins introduced her to William. They went roller skating. Three straight nights.

They did not see each other again for almost five years. Dottie's dad had moved the family to St. Louis. He opened a shoe repair store on Delmar Boulevard. William had come to St. Louis, too. Each heard through friends that the other was in St. Louis, but they did not make connections. They got together again when they were both visiting Sikeston.

Three months after they reconnected, they were married. Their wedding was on Halloween in 1953.

Their first son was born on Halloween in 1954. Their next son was born on Halloween in 1955. Their third son was born in April 1957. Their daughter was born in January 1959. Their names are Mike, Bill, Bob and Enola, who was called Gay.

William got a job as a union painter. The family lived in a mobile home in St. Charles County. William was gone a lot of the time working. He was afraid he wasn't communicating with his kids. He decided to write them a letter. One night in 1964, he put his thoughts on paper. It was not fancy paper – three sheets, and they didn't match.

"It has occurred to me for sometime that I have never taken the time to have a real good talk with you boys and Gay. Forgive me for not doing that, but day to day occurrences get good intentions sidetracked. And it seems I never get to do the things I would like to have done.

"First of all, there is one thing I would ask you to consider before you commit yourselves to any circumstance. And that is, ask yourself, is this the right thing to do? Would God have me do this?

"Your dad would ask you to always give your fellow man respect, love, honesty. These, you will find, are not always given, and sometimes not returned. Even as you read these words, there will be times in your life in which that is all they will be, Words. But these three words are the basis for other words you will come to know the meaning of. Such as kindness, compassion, loyalty, sincerity and generosity.

"Ignorance is a terribly hopeless way of life. Knowledge and faith in God can change any man, any circumstance. I can see from the short time I have lived that these things are fact and truth.

"I can see and know that you boys and Gay have been taught kindness, love and honesty by your Mother. I am sorry I can't take much credit for these qualities. I desired that you have them more than anything. And I hope they will grow in depth as you grow older.

"You will find occasions in your life that these words will not do something for you. They won't feed you when you are hungry. They won't give you material comfort when you expect you should have it. But if you pray to God for wisdom to use these words, God will answer your prayers. Learn well my sons and daughter.

"Your Dad, Wm. Hill"

Thirty-four years later, on Father's Day in 1998, Mike wrote his father a response.

"The letter you wrote was much more than words. It was a lesson about love and a good set of directions for life. Like most men, I seem to have a problem occasionally about not reading directions. Thank you, Dad, for loving us enough to bother to write down those directions. They were a big help and every time I go back to them I go the right way. Happy Father's Day."

By the way, all the kids went the right way. Everybody is doing fine. There are eight grandkids and 14 great-grandkids.

The two letters were first published in a Father's Day story by Jason Lee in the St. Charles County Journal in 2004. Lee talked to William Hill, who told him that he thought a letter was more meaningful than a talk. Kids don't listen to preaching, Hill said.

William died in October 2006, six days before Halloween, which has always been a special holiday for the Hills. As is Father's Day.

"We all miss him so much," Dottie told me when I visited last week.

Fortunately, they still have his letter.

FEBRUARY 2, 1994

Great expectations: Baby Jesus is anticipated shortly at West County home

In a quiet middle-class neighborhood in west St. Louis County, people are convinced that the baby Jesus will be coming on Christmas Eve.

He will be coming, people say, to a house on Sparrowhawk Court. That's where Ted Laspe used to live. Laspe died in October. He was only 47, but he had been on a disability pension since 1990. He had had epilepsy and diabetes since childhood, but he had been in relatively good health until 1988, when he had open-heart surgery. After that, his health went steadily downhill.

Not that he spent his time complaining. He certainly didn't. As talkative as he was – and he was the kind of fellow who would strike up conversations with strangers in the grocery store – he seldom talked about his own troubles.

Maybe that's because he was aware that many people had more severe problems. After his retirement, he spent a good deal of time looking after the neighborhood's shut-ins. He was always available to do errands or take people shopping. He used to visit one elderly woman just to watch a television game show. He knew how much she needed company.

In fact, there was so much to do that he would sometimes get frazzled. It happened every Christmas season. He'd be baking cookies, talking about things he could do for organizations that helped needy children, talking about making Christmas decorations, and finally he'd just throw up his hands, and turn to his wife, Liz.

"We're going to have to cancel Christmas!" he'd say.

His two stepdaughters would laugh and laugh.

He had an old plastic Nativity scene he used to put in front of his house. It was very standard stuff. Three wise men, two sheep, one camel, one donkey, one shepherd, and, of course, Joseph and Mary. All were huddled around the crib that held baby Jesus. It went up well before Christmas, and it stayed up well after Christmas.

Last January, when Laspe finally went out to take it down, baby Jesus was gone from its crib. In its place was a note. "Dear Ted, On vacation – Be back Christmas Eve of 1994." Laspe thought it was the darnedest thing. He figured that a neighbor had done it.

Laspe, of course, was the sort of fellow who talked to all his neighbors. For example, even though he didn't have a dog, he used to save bones, and whenever a neighbor walked a dog past Laspe's house, Laspe rushed out with a bone. After a while, the dogs stopped of their own accord at Laspe's house.

At any rate, Laspe talked to all his neighbors, and they all denied knowing anything about the missing baby Jesus.

The first postcard came in February. It was from Colorado.

"Having a great time. The mountains are wonderful – close to heaven! Gotta go. Hi to Liz. Love, Jesus."

A week later, another postcard came, also from Colorado. Two weeks after that, another postcard came, this one from Phoenix. The following week, Laspe got a post card from California.

A couple of weeks after that, a postcard came from Wisconsin, and that was followed by a card from Minnesota, and that was followed by a card from Iowa, and then one from Arkansas. All were signed, "Love Jesus." Most promised something like, "See you on Christmas Eve." Although the messages were always similar, the handwriting was not always identical. Somebody was playing an elaborate game.

In August, the first photographs came. There were pictures of Laspe's baby Jesus in the mountains of Utah, pictures of baby Jesus sitting against a plaque in Ogden, Utah.

Laspe, his family and his friends were beside themselves.

"Every time he got a new postcard, he'd rush over," said Mark Czechut, one of his best friends. "We'd try to figure out who could be doing this."

The postcards kept coming. From New York to California. More photographs came. The babyJesus was on an airplane. A flight attendant was holding him.

In October, Laspe died.

A postcard came addressed to Liz.

"Took some time off from my vacation to make sure Ted got settled in. He's just fine. See you soon. Love Jesus."

The day after Thanksgiving, Liz and her daughters put the Nativity scene out. The crib, of course, was empty.

But the people on and around Sparrowhawk Court are quite convinced that it won't be empty long. Sometime on Christmas Eve, they wager, while the children of the world are looking skyward, dreaming of presents and watching for reindeer, the baby Jesus will find its way back into the crib that sits in front of the home of a man who truly knew how to celebrate Christmas.

And there are those who say that Ted Laspe, who always loved a good joke, will be there, as well, albeit unseen, when his family and friends gather around the crib to celebrate the return of the baby Jesus.

JANUARY 7, 1991

Grinning and baring an intrepid dad's life of the skids

Saturday morning, and the children were already watching cartoons. I fixed some coffee and threw open the back door to let the dogs out.

The fat dog slipped on the ice and ended up on her back, like a bug. As she tried to right herself, I stood at the top of the stairs laughing. My laughter attracted the kids.

"Look at Tia," I said. "Hahahaha."

Finally, she righted herself and threw me a hateful glance.

After letting the dogs back in, I decided to get the paper. I thought briefly about putting on my clothes, or at least my shoes, but decided not to bother. After all, I was wearing my robe.

Out the front door I went.

No wonder Tia had slipped. A sheet of ice was covering everything.

Gingerly, I made my way down the steps. Gingerly, I crossed the lawn, and very carefully I went down the small incline that leads to the sidewalk.

I picked up the paper and headed back.

But I couldn't get back up the mountain.

At least that's what the incline seemed like. It's only about three feet, and it never seemed particularly steep before, but I couldn't get back up.

Meanwhile, my bare feet were beginning to get very cold.

Again, I tried to get up the incline, and again, I slipped back. My feet were now very cold, too cold. I sat down on the ice-covered sidewalk, and rubbed my feet.

I gave myself a pep talk and tried again to get up the incline. One step up, and then I slid back down.

If Jack London had ever written a script for Chevy Chase, this would have been it.

When I looked up at the window — if only my wife were aware of what was happening — the only face that was visible belonged to Tia. She was sitting on the couch, watching me. She loves to sit on the couch and look outside. As far as she's concerned, it's exercise.

Perhaps the cold was beginning to get to me, but it looked as if she were laughing.

She was laughing!

No, she wasn't. It was another face that was laughing. Two other faces. The children!

I hugged myself to pantomime that I was cold. I sat on the sidewalk and rubbed my feet. I hugged myself again.

Now the children were applauding!

In a sense, this was my fault. Several days earlier, the children had complained about the cold, and to show them what a He-Man their father is, I ran outside without a shirt on. I danced around in the cold while they stood at the window cheering.

Obviously, that had been a bad idea. Now, in my moment of need, the kids thought I was trying to amuse them.

I was beginning to get very, very cold.

Desperation led to an idea. If I were to take my robe off, and use it as a carpet, perhaps I could get up the incline.

But if I were to take off my robe, I'd be really cold.

Furthermore, I'd be opening myself to a criminal charge. After all, I'd be exposing myself.

And what if I were to slip, and knock myself out? Without my robe on, I'd be a goner in minutes.

Then I'd really be in trouble. I know a lot of prosecutors, and I know how they work. In my mind, I heard the closing argument in the case against me.

"He's charged with exposing himself. And what does the death certificate say he died from? Exposure!"

I'd be charged with the same thing that killed me. I wouldn't have a chance.

I didn't want to put my family through that ordeal. I struggled to my feet again and took a step up the hill. Back down I slid.

I glanced back up at the window, and wonder of wonders, the children's laughter had awakened my wife. I was saved!

But wait. A closer look revealed that something was wrong. My wife was crying.

I stared at the window. She was crying because she was laughing so hard. Obviously, she didn't know how desperate my situation was.

I hugged myself.

She applauded!

I sat back down on the sidewalk to rub my feet. Moments later, my wife came out. She was wearing her coat, and her boots, and she was carrying towels.

From the top of the incline, she threw me the towels, and I managed to crawl up the hill.

I walked into the house, and the children applauded.

"Good show!" said my daughter.

"Funny!" said my son.

Tia, who looked vaguely disappointed, rolled over and went to sleep.

SEPTEMBER 7, 2008

Seasons fly by in the blink of an eye

The rain stopped Thursday night, and Friday morning it was autumn. There was nothing gradual about the change in seasons.

Of course, it had been obvious for a while that fall was coming. Even before Labor Day, children had started going past my house each morning on their way to school. Sometimes I'd be outside and I'd chat with the parents as they walked past. I can usually be called upon to say something trite. "It goes by in the blink of an eye, " is one of my standards.

When we moved into our house, my wife was pregnant with our first child. As the years went by, older neighbors, whose kids already were gone, would say similar things to me. Now most of those older neighbors are gone, replaced by the young parents who go past my house. It is easy for a sentimental person to get morose as the seasons change.

On Friday morning, I saw a monarch butterfly in our backyard. Now if ever a creature had reason to be morose at the coming of fall, it's a monarch butterfly.

Monarch butterflies fly to the mountains of Michoacán in central Mexico for the winter. Imagine that. A monarch butterfly weighs about an ounce. What happens if it hits a headwind? A goose is big enough to just plow through a headwind, but a butterfly? Yet they come from as far north as Canada into the Mexican mountains. That's about a 2,500-mile trip.

What's more, it's an intergenerational trip. The butterflies that winter in Mexico never have been there before. They are the descendants of butterflies who spent the previous winter in the mountains. Yet scientists think they not only return to the same few groves, but maybe even the same trees as did their relatives. They hang from the oyamel fir trees in huge bunches. They mate in the groves. The males then die, and the females make it north to the U.S. Gulf of Mexico states before laying eggs and dying themselves.

I decided to see the butterflies for myself last year. My family and I were in Texas visiting relatives at Christmas. My daughter had to get back to California where she teaches high school biology. My wife had to get back to St. Louis for work. My son was on winter break from the University of Wisconsin and still had about a week before he had to be back at school. Let's go to Mexico, I said. Maybe we can see the butterflies in Michoacán.

Jack and I flew to Mexico City at night and turned around the next morning and caught a flight north to Zacatecas, which is the northernmost of the silver cities. We stayed there for two days. We went to a wonderful saloon called Las Quince Letras – the Fifteen Letters – and met Alfonso Lopez Monriel. I was wearing a cap from the city of Derry in Northern Ireland. Alfonso told us he had been in Northern Ireland during the Troubles. Which side were you on? I asked. "I am an atheist, " he said, "but a Catholic one."

Jack and I took a nine-hour bus ride to Morelia, the capital of Michóacán. We tried to catch a bus to Angangueo, the closest town to the most famous of the butterfly reserves, El Rosario. But the road was out, and we ended up in Zitácuaro, which is the city closest to the most recently opened reserve, Cerro Pellón.

The entrance to the reserve is next to a cluster of houses. The man at the gate asked if we wanted to rent horses. How long a hike is it? we asked. About two hours, he said. We chose to hike. You'll need a guide, he said, and he called over to a young man from the cluster of houses.

Did I say a young man? I should have said a mountain goat. He led us up a footpath that sometimes disappeared. I became exhausted. Up and up we went. Finally, we reached a clearing. There were monarch butterflies. Not as many as I had hoped for, but lots of them. It was a bit like being in a butterfly house at a zoo.

Perfect, I said, and collapsed.

No, a little farther, said our guide.

We went around the bend. Thousands and thousands of monarch butterflies were hanging from the fir trees like living ornaments. Butterflies were joining the clumps and leaving the clumps. They were flying around. They were all over.

It was a spectacular sight, but a little sad, too. The males would not make it out of the grove. The females would not make it all the way home.

I thought about that as I saw the butterfly in my yard. "It goes by in the blink of an eye, " I said to him.

OCTOBER 24, 1999

If I could spend an hour in the past, I think I know just what I would do

I brought a copy of my daughter's birth certificate with us Friday morning when I took her to the state license bureau on South Kingshighway. She was going to take the test to get her driver's permit.

The birth certificate wasn't enough. We needed her Social Security card. So home we went, and I rushed downstairs to the dresser in which I keep the family's important papers. It's not much of a file system. There is a folder titled "House." Another titled "Insurance." Another marked "Manuals and Warranties." Another titled "Credit Cards." All these attempts, mostly in vain, to keep our modern lives straight.

There are also two files marked "Personal." They could just as well be titled "Miscellaneous." It would be in one of these folders, each bulging with papers, that a Social Security card might be found. I quickly began rummaging through the first folder.

Almost immediately I slowed down. Birth certificates, death certificates, report cards, old photos, three generations worth of military discharge papers, even a very crudely hand-drawn Father's Day card. To A Loving Father. From Billy.

Oh, to time-travel. Not back to the time of dinosaurs, or the time of Christ, or the Civil War. To just go back in your own life. To spend an hour as the person you once were.

I'd spend an hour as a child, back with the family as it once was. My dad was tough and strong and competent. He was an electrician who worked outside in the Chicago weather. My mom was fun-loving and delicate. Her mom, who lived with us, was an elfin figure who had been born in Belfast. Then, of course, there was my sister. She was a golden child. Too good to be true.

All of them are long gone. Oh, to have just an hour again in those innocent days before any of the catastrophes befell us.

I wouldn't stop with the family. I'd spend an hour back in high school. I was a member in good standing of the B crowd. Maybe we gave ourselves too much credit. Maybe others thought of us as the C crowd. What does it matter?

I'd spend an hour with some college buddies, and for sure, I'd time-travel back to the Marine Corps. I'd lean back and listen to the fellows talking about what they'd do when they got back to the states. Back to the world, is the way it was phrased.

Then I'd spend an hour in Arizona in my post-service days. My pals and I would probably be smoking some cheap, low-grade pot, or maybe we'd be hanging out at the local diner, drinking coffee at 3 a.m. It felt good to do that! We were letting people know that there was no place we had to be any time soon.

I came here almost 20 years ago, and I'd time-travel back to my early days on the paper. Maybe spend a few minutes in the newsroom with friends who have since retired, and then zip over to the police station and the homicide office. I'd chat with the likes of John Roussin and Wayne Bender. Rich Kurre from the Globe would be there, too.

All of these things and more went through my mind as I looked for my daughter's Social Security card. Faces of a hundred friends danced before me. And then it hit me. A sudden realization almost knocked me over.

We are time-traveling. The present is the past before we know it. Turn around and the moment is gone. This instant is already over.

Now what would I do if I could revisit past moments? In every example I cited, I would let people know how much I appreciate them. How I'd hug my mother!

What words of love I'd have for my sister and my father!

I wouldn't be as gushy with my friends, but if I could go back at will, I'd lean over and gently punch a shoulder here, say a kind word there. I'd probably get some strange looks, but what the heck.

Once I had the necessary paperwork, my daughter and I headed back to the license bureau. I drove slowly, trying to stretch the time, but I realized that you can't stretch time.

The most you can do is realize that you're time-traveling. I tried not to think of my daughter driving, and how that means that she's growing up, and how I'll soon be seeing the taillights as she drives away from me. Enjoy the moment, I told myself, and I did, just as I'm enjoying this moment, except that I miss it already.

APRIL 10, 1996

I'm on a roll: Now, from the ballpark, on to bullfights

In May 1986, I wrote a thoughtful essay published in this newspaper. The essay was critical of Busch Stadium.

The walls need to come in a bit, I wrote, and most importantly, the Astroturf needs to be replaced with grass. At the time, my ideas were ridiculed as the rantings of a transplanted Cubs fan, but now, 10 years later, my suggestions have become reality, and everybody seems to agree that the changes I proposed have greatly improved the old park.

As long as I am basking in this kind of public approval, it seems like a good time to revisit some other ideas that I have championed.

First is the matter of the bulls.

We would become the only city in this country to have bullfights. This would be a tremendous tourist draw, and if there were to be some outraged animal rights protesters, let me remind the restaurant and hotel interests that protesters have to eat and sleep, too.

What's more, we wouldn't stop at merely having bullfights. We'd have an annual – maybe a monthly – running of the bulls, just like they have in Pamplona, Spain.

I first proposed this idea in 1993. Let me quote from that column.

"We'll run the bulls right down Washington Avenue. We'll release them out of big vans, just west of Jefferson Avenue. What a magnificent sight it will be as the bulls, framed by tall buildings on either side, thunder down the street toward the convention center.

"Real estate values along Washington will skyrocket. People will rent the vacant lofts to have a bird's-eye of the mayhem.

"Can't you just picture the deputies hauling the civic leaders on to the street? Our leaders look nervously at the giant vans holding the bulls while in the lofts, the crowd screams, "Hobble them!'"

You see, while adventurous tourists would be allowed to participate, various civic leaders would be forced to participate. That is, whichever public officials were in disfavor at the time.

For instance, if a bull-running were to take place today, we'd almost certainly see Mavis Thompson, the St. Louis circuit clerk, galloping down Washington Avenue trying to stay ahead of the charging bulls. Thompson, of course, recently tried to justify the fact that she had overspent her travel budget by declaring that she was not just a circuit clerk, but an ambassador.

"Just pretend you're in Spain!" the crowd would shout as she raced down the street.

Thompson would be an easy choice, but what about other civic leaders? Who would be empowered to decide which ones had to participate?

The bull-running czar!

Since the whole thing is my idea, I would serve. Compensation could be worked out.

Another idea I have long championed concerns fashion. Several times I have suggested that St. Louis and St. Louis County encourage men to wear shorts in the summer.

For one thing, it makes sense. I've been in cities in the tropics where men wear shorts to work, and it's just as hot and humid here. More importantly, it would give us something we're lacking — a unique style. We'd be different.

Plus, it would be a fun thing.

We could have a special local holiday celebrating the summer solstice, after which men would be expected to wear shorts to work. Then, during the rest of the summer, politicians would wear shorts, cops would wear shorts, visiting dignitaries would wear shorts, everybody would wear shorts.

Tourists would get warning tickets if they wore long pants.

Bullfighting and shorts. Both make sense. They'd really put us on the map.

I have suggested both of these ideas before. Sadly, neither idea has been taken seriously.

But hey, when I first proposed revamping Busch Stadium, nobody listened. Finally, though, 10 years after I began my campaign, the changes were made.

Now, the city is thrilled.

"McClellan was right. This is a lot nicer," people are saying.

In fact, if you go to the game this afternoon, look around. If you like what you see, if you think I was right, let your imagination take over.

Think about a hot August day. You're wearing shorts, walking down Washington Avenue, jockeying for position behind the barricades. The sidewalk is loaded with tourists. The swells are hanging out the windows of the lofts.

You buy a program to see which civic leaders will be running.

Far to the west on Jefferson Avenue, the vans are pulling up. The bulls are snorting.

Only in St. Louis.

FEBRUARY 5, 2014

In a long work life well lived, time to check out

Edward Smith was a sharecropper in the Bootheel. He liked to gamble. He was shot and killed in 1930. Apparently, it was during or right after a card game. Maybe he'd just won some money. Maybe there'd been an argument. Details are sketchy. Edward was survived by his wife, Hattie, and their five children.

The middle child was Bill. He was 5 when his dad was killed.

Hattie and her kids moved in with her father. He was a sharecropper, too. Hattie died of cancer four years later. Her father died three years after her.

Bill was 12. He was sent to St. Louis to live with his mother's younger sister, Evelyn Thompson.

He finished grade school in St. Louis. Then he went to Washington Technical High School at 19th and Franklin, a school for black kids. He met Ruby Harris there. They became a couple. They talked about marriage. Ruby said she couldn't cook. Bill had done some cooking back in the Bootheel, but he didn't see himself being the family cook. He asked Ruby if she was willing to learn to cook. She said yes.

They were married in 1947.

Bill had hopes of becoming a machinist, but this was a strong union town, and the union was not accepting blacks for apprenticeships. So Bill got a job as a laborer at a meat packing company. Then he was promoted to a job curing bacon. Then he became a meat-cutter. But the company merged with another packing company, and Bill's job was eliminated.

By then, Ruby was doing well. She had her own beauty parlor on Page Avenue.

Bill got a job as a warehouse man with Rawlings. That seemed a great fit. Bill was an amateur baseball player of some renown. He played in several Negro leagues. He stayed at Rawlings for about 12 years until the warehouse operations moved to Springfield, Mo.

He was out of work again, but not for long. He got a job as maintenance man for the Most Blessed Sacrament Church on North Kingshighway. He worked there for a couple of years until a friend told him that Local 1 of the International Brotherhood of Electrical Workers was looking for a maintenance worker. He got the job and stayed there for 11 years until he retired in 1991. He was 66.

By then, he and Ruby had raised two kids. They owned a home in Richmond Heights. Owned it outright. Bill did some gardening. Turnips, collard greens, okra, tomatoes. He did some volunteer work for his church, Little Flower Catholic Church. But some days he felt like working again.

One day in 1995 he heard an advertisement on the radio for Schnucks. The ad said the grocery chain was looking for workers. It mentioned that senior citizens were welcome to apply. Bill did. He was hired. He did a couple of weeks at the Ladue Crossing store, and then he moved over to the then-unopened store on Clayton Road in Richmond Heights.

He helped with the cleanup as the construction crews put the final touches on the store. It opened in August 1995.

Bill was a bagger. He was 70 years old.

Bagging is most often a young person's job. A starter job. An older person might well be defensive about having a starter job, but Bill was always able to bag groceries while maintaining the dignity that comes with age. And he seemed to do so unconsciously, which is, of course, the only way dignity can truly be maintained.

Years went by.

He was perhaps the most recognizable person in the store, and as he bagged, he chatted easily with the customers, many of whom he had come to know.

Several times, he was asked if he'd like to move up to a checkout position. Bill was not interested. Last month, after almost 20 years as a bagger, Bill retired.

I visited him last week. Twenty years is practically a career. Why had he not wanted to become a checker?

He said he didn't have the temperament for checking. That surprised me. He always seemed calm and collected. He laughed and said there wasn't much pressure on baggers. "I knew what I was doing, and I never aggravated anybody," he said.

Besides, he liked his job, but his life was filled with other things. He has two grown kids, a grandson, his church. He's active in the Knights of Columbus. He's on an advisory board for Big Brothers, Big Sisters. He doesn't serve as a Big Brother to any kids these days, but he's still in touch with at least one of his Little Brothers, who is, by now, a grown man. He was coming over for dinner on the day I visited. Maybe their relationship had stayed strong because of what they had in common. "His father was murdered, too, " Bill said.

By the way, they were going to have beef stew. Ingredients from Schnucks. Somebody else did the bagging.

MAY 26, 2013

In Vietnam, a tale of two Marines

When college didn't work out, Cottrell Fox joined the Marine Corps. That didn't shock anybody who knew him in Webster Groves. His two older brothers had been Marines. In fact, one of them had already been in and out of Vietnam by the time Fox got there in February 1967.

Fox was in a CAP (Combined Action Program) unit. A Marine rifle squad of 11 or 12 men and a Navy corpsman lived in a village. They were reinforced by a Vietnamese militia platoon, generally made up of villagers who were too old or too young to be drafted. The idea was to deny the enemy the sanctuary of the village.

Fox's village was Loc Dien, about 14 miles south of Hue. It was on Highway One and protected a strategic bridge across the Truoi River. Although the CAP unit was small, it was covered by artillery from Phu Bai. Also, Marine rifle companies operating in the area were available if needed. At least, that was the theory.

In reality, the CAP units were sometimes out on a long, narrow limb.

The truth of that became evident at the onset of the Tet Offensive. In the early morning hours of Jan. 31, 1968, a North Vietnamese Army battalion attacked the CAP compound at Loc Dien. The fighting was fierce. Fox was wounded several times. A grenade smacked into his head, rolled away and exploded. He was shot in the arm at close range. The Marines called artillery in on their own position. Air burst rounds. They hunkered in their bunkers as the shrapnel rained down.

Fox survived, but his war was over.

He was taken by medevac to the Philippines and then to Hawaii. He spent several weeks in a hospital in Honolulu. Many of the fellows he was with were from Hotel Company, 2nd Battalion, 5th Regiment. That had been one of the companies operating in the area around Loc Dien. During Tet, the company had been mauled in the meat-grinder at Hue.

When Fox finished his two-year hitch, he returned to college. He eventually graduated from the University of Missouri.

Meanwhile, of course, the war went on. In September 1968, Peter Mary Nee arrived inVietnam and joined Hotel Company, 2nd Battalion, 5th Regiment.

Nee was from Ireland. He was born on Aug. 15 – the Feast Day of the Assumption of the Blessed Virgin Mary – which explains his middle name. He was from the tiny village of Bunahown, near the town of Cashel in an area along the Atlantic known as Connemara. He came to the U.S. in his early teens. He wanted to become a citizen. He joined the Marine Corps.

He planned to go to college after the service. Perhaps he would have become a writer. Actually, he already was one. He wrote poetry.

"My mind was not a mind but a canyon

where thoughts and ideas bounded

from wall to wall.

My heart was not a heart but a bowl,

which when filled, cracked and

allowed its content to flow away."

He was wounded in January 1969 but soon returned to his friends in Hotel Company. He was a squad leader in this First Platoon. He was much respected, a corpsman, Dennis "Doc Kuff" Kuftic, recalled in an email.

"I loved Peter. He had more personality, good humor and charm than any person I've met before or since. He could call you an idiot in a way that you'd think it was a compliment. I remember him telling me he was Irish and not an American. I asked him then why the hell would he join the Marines. He told me, "Cause it was green.' He was brave, bold, confident and an adventurer. No one ever questioned him. You could tell he knew what he was doing."

Jay Peterson, a radio operator, recalled Nee's sense of humor. He said Nee loved the ice cream bars that would occasionally arrive with resupply.

"Peter was constantly saying with his Irish accent that we would be getting ice cream with the next resupply – as if saying it with a positive attitude would make it happen."

On the last day of March 1969, Hotel Company was on an operation in an area called the Arizona Territory. As Nee's squad approached a tree line, someone spotted an NVA soldier. He ducked into the trees, Corpsman Kuftic remembered.

"We of course went after him. We were in single file and entered the tree line in the same spot the enemy entered. Peter was the third man back. I was the fifth. In front of the tree line was a drainage ditch. Peter and the rest of the men up front jumped over it. For some reason, I stepped down into it just as the explosion went off."

It could have been a booby trap or an RPG. Either way, Nee was killed.

Later that day, the company was resupplied. They got ice cream.

JUNE 18, 2012

KMOX's relocation just a sign of times

A small item in Friday's newspaper noted that CBS Radio St. Louis is consolidating its three local stations into one building.

"KMOX-AM, KEZK-FM and Y98 will move into the Park Pacific, a mixed-use office and condo building at the corner of Olive Street and Tucker Boulevard, according to market manager John Sheehan."

There was a time – and not so long ago – when this would have been unthinkable.

KMOX was at One Memorial Drive. It was there because it was a good location. Its studios overlooked the Gateway Arch. It could have found cheaper digs, but it was KMOX, and it was run by Robert Hyland, and he was not a "market manager." He was the general manager of a 50,000-watt radio station that considered itself the finest radio station in the country.

And more, too. "We are the city's third newspaper," he used to say.

In those days, there were two newspapers in St. Louis – the Post-Dispatch and the Globe-Democrat.

That was the situation when I got here in 1980. I interviewed at both papers. I failed a writing test at the Globe-Democrat but was hired by the Post-Dispatch to do listings in the Calendar section.

That was not a big job, but I was in the media community. I had occasion to visit One Memorial Drive. More precisely, I had occasion to visit saloons and restaurants near One Memorial Drive.

What fun it was. The KMOX people shared their building with Channel 4 television, and with the ad agency D'Arcy-MacManus & Masius.

That agency had had the brewery account for decades. The ad guys would sit at lunch with a bottle of whatever brand they were working on – Natural Light, Michelob, Budweiser – sitting in front of their martinis. Maybe it was at one of those lunches that one of them came up with "This Bud's for you."

By the way, the KMOX people could drink with the D'Arcy people, and when it came to storytelling, the KMOX people were in a league of their own.

Anne Keefe, who was a mentor to many of the young radio people, told of the time she left the station and happened upon a small child, alone, standing at the light about to try to cross Broadway. She ran over and scooped the child up just as he was ready to step off the curb. He squirmed in her arms and turned his face toward her. It was an old face, and angry, too.

He said he was attending a convention of little people at a nearby hotel.

Anne smiled and said, "Welcome to St. Louis," as she put him down.

I suspect the young radio people liked Anne not only because she was kind to them, but because she was in awe of nobody, not even Hyland.

He was larger than life. Consumed with the radio station, people said. The overnighters and early morning people said he would call at the strangest hours. It was as if he were always listening.

Maybe that's what you have to do if you want a world-class radio station, and that is exactly what he wanted – and what he got.

All local, too. A radio station by and for St. Louisans. That was important to Hyland. Another advantage – he could control everything.

The ratings were the stuff of legend. KMOX was always the No. 1 station. Grown-up radio, we used to call it.

As I mentioned, Hyland also took great pride in his news operation.

But, of course, things change. The Globe-Democrat went out of business. D'Arcy moved to New York. Hyland died, and KMOX, like this newspaper, became a shadow of its former self.

We have fewer reporters, and our circulation numbers are down. KMOX is no longer all-local, and no longer the No. 1 station in St. Louis. Its numbers are a fraction of what they once were.

I have never heard of Sheehan, the market manager, but I would not blame him for the decline of KMOX.

People in that industry tell me it's all complicated. There are a zillion options these days. People might listen to CDs in their cars. Or maybe iPods. Or maybe even radio you have to subscribe to.

A marketing guy told me, "Many young people couldn't even name a radio station today."

In that sense, it was not big news that KMOX is leaving One Memorial Drive.

I'm sure the move will save money, which is why businesses do things these days.

But there was a time when saving money was not always the most important goal, and it is the end of that time that rates more than a mention in the Business section.

JANUARY 1, 2014

La Russa must think other fans still care

As regular readers know, I grew up on the south side of Chicago. That is White Sox territory. But my people were Protestants in Northern Ireland and therefore accustomed to being out of step with their neighbors. They became Cub fans.

My friends rooted for the White Sox. I am still in touch with a couple of them. I called one this weekend. He loves the White Sox.

"You must be celebrating for Tony," I said.

"Tony who?" said my friend.

"Tony La Russa," I replied. "He's going into the Hall of Fame without a logo."

My friend said he had heard something about that. It had been mentioned in connection with Greg Maddux's decision to not have a logo. The Maddux decision has apparently been much discussed in Chicago. Maddux was with the Cubs and then the Braves and then came back to the Cubs. He had a lot of success in Atlanta so people figured he'd go in as a Brave. So yes, people in Chicago have talked about Maddux. But La Russa? My friend wanted to know why anybody in Chicago would care about his decision to go in without a logo.

"Because he's honoring White Sox fans," I explained.

La Russa managed three teams — the White Sox, the Oakland A's and the Cardinals. In a press release, he said, "It's the totality of the success of each of those three teams that led me to Cooperstown, so I am choosing not to feature a logo so that fans of all clubs can celebrate this honor with me." I explained that to my friend, and asked if he was celebrating with Tony.

"He was fired here. I was glad to see him go," said my friend.

Well, yes, he was run out of Chicago, but that doesn't mean the fans don't remember him fondly. Sometimes popular managers get fired. I can't think of too many offhand, but I'm sure there have been some.

"Well, he's celebrating with you whether you like it or not, " I said.

"That's crazy, " said my friend.

One of my wife's sisters lives in northern California. Her husband is a lawyer in Oakland. I called them. My brother-in-law wasn't home, but my sister-in-law knows a lot about sports. She has two sons.

I told her I was writing a story about Tony La Russa going into the Hall of Fame without a logo. I asked if she had heard much talk about that. "None, " she said.

That's not surprising. I checked the Oakland Tribune website last week. There were a couple of stories, but no comments. The decision by La Russa has not created much of a stir in the Bay area.

Of course, it's been almost 20 years since La Russa managed in Oakland. He left after the 1995 season.

Actually, the only place La Russa's decision has created any kind of a stir is here. Fans in St. Louis expected him to go into the Hall of Fame as a Cardinal. He managed here longer than any manager before him. He managed here longer than he managed anywhere else. He won more games here than anywhere else. More World Series titles.

His record in Chicago was not Hall of Fame material. He won 522 games and lost 510. He did better in Oakland — his team went to the World Series three straight years — but frankly, that success comes with an asterisk. That Oakland team was led by the "Bash Brothers, " Jose Canseco and Mark McGwire. We now know that was the dawn of Steroid Era. The Oakland team was playing with a stacked deck.

La Russa punched his ticket to the Hall of Fame in St. Louis. He had great success here. Even his critics have to admit that by the time he got here, players everywhere were using. Nobody had an advantage. In a lawless era, his teams flourished. After things got sort of cleaned up, his teams still flourished.

Because of his long record of success here, it seemed natural that he'd go in as a Cardinal. After all, his number was retired here. It wasn't retired in Oakland. It wasn't retired in Chicago.

A lot of people here see La Russa's decision as a snub. That thinking has roots. La Russa managed here for 16 years, but never lived here. He never made much of an effort to connect with the community. He acted like the midnight man stuck in the 9 o'clock town.

That attitude stung because St. Louisans have an inferiority complex. There is nothing snazzy about St. Louis. We're a comfortable shoe of a place. We are always ready to be snubbed.

Bernie Miklasz wrote last week that he does not believe La Russa is snubbing anybody. He knows La Russa, so I'll defer to him.

Actually, that makes the story a sad one, and La Russa becomes a tragic figure. He thinks the fans in Chicago and Oakland would have been hurt if he went into the Hall as a Cardinal. Truth is, the only fans who care are right here.

MARCH 16, 2014

Leaving 4th Street, but not the memories

Doug and Dee Donahue moved to Tucson 50 years ago into a house on Fourth Street near the University of Arizona. The oldest of their four daughters was 12.

Several years later, she enrolled in the university. She did all right, but she was not a serious student. Her father decided that maybe she ought to try something else. Somebody told him that dental hygiene was a fine profession for a young woman. He learned there was a dental hygiene program at a community college in Phoenix. He scheduled an interview for his daughter.

He told her she had an interview to get into a dental hygiene program and she thought, "Well, why not?"

Perhaps this willingness to accept changed circumstances came from her father. Doug grew up in California wanting to be a sportswriter. Then World War II came along and he joined the Navy. The Navy decided he had an aptitude for science and sent him to Park College in Parkville, Mo., to take science classes. He stuck with that after the war and became a nuclear physicist.

His oldest daughter graduated from the dental hygiene program in Phoenix and moved into an apartment next to mine. I had long hair and a black pug named Primo. I had covered the floor in my apartment with sample squares of carpet. Different colors and patterns. A fortune teller had recently warned her that she would soon meet an unkempt young man with long hair, and while the fortune teller had said nothing about a pug or carpet squares, she figured I was probably the aforementioned young man. Oh well.

We eventually got married in the living room of the house on Fourth Street. I wrote the ceremony. It was traditional until it reached the part at which the minister said, "If anyone knows why this couple should not be joined in holy matrimony, let him speak now or forever hold his peace." At that point, I had a friend stand up and say, "They've been happy living together. I don't see why they should get married." It shocked everybody, especially Doug and Dee.

We had our reception in the backyard. So did the other sisters when they got married.

Photos of the various wedding parties hang in the house now. They are two or three years apart, so that nobody seems to have aged much, but in the later photos, there are toddlers.

Then there are photos of these toddlers — and others that followed — as they began to grow up. Many of these photos were taken at the house on Fourth Street because the sisters — and their younger brother — were scattered from New York to California, from St. Louis to San Antonio, and it made sense to gather for the holidays in Tucson.

Occasionally, other events brought us to Tucson. In 1988, Doug's lab at the university was one of three labs to carbon date the Shroud of Turin. The two other labs were at Oxford and Zurich. The labs had agreed not to release the results individually. Doug had invited Harry Gove, a physicist from the University of Rochester, to observe. Gove had had a poor relationship with the scientific adviser to the bishop of Turin, and his lab had been excluded from the testing.

I was waiting for them at the house on Fourth Street when they returned from the lab. Neither of them mentioned the results, but as we had a drink on the porch, I sensed — correctly — from Gove that the results were not what Turin would have wanted.

Mostly, though, the house was the scene of parties. Loud and boisterous. The sort you would expect from a family of Irish descent. The sisters teasing each other — usually in good humor — about childhood transgressions, and their children exchanging glances as if to ask, "Are these really our moms?" It was like living in a book — The Sisters Donahue.

Not long ago, Dee fell. She was not hurt badly, but it was clear that living on the second floor, climbing up and down steps, was not a good idea. For that matter, the house required too much maintenance. Doug and Dee moved into an apartment for senior citizens.

My son, one of the toddlers in those wedding party photos, moved in as kind of a caretaker. But that was a temporary thing. Then one of the sisters moved back to Tucson. But again, her move was temporary. She has a life — and a house — of her own.

My wife and I visited Tucson and stayed in the house on Fourth Street this past week. It will go on the market next month. If I could, I'd warn the potential buyers: Don't be surprised if it's haunted, but don't worry, either. The ghosts are all laughing.

SEPTEMBER 25, 2013

Man wanted to go on his own terms

James Wesley Green was a saloon keeper. He had a string of bars and five wives. He had three children with his first, and he reared them with the help of the four others. When his daughter, Sherri, was grown, she used to tease him. "One more and you'll have your pall-bearers."

When he died in 1990, his kids inherited his final tavern, Jim Green's Saloon. It was on Woodson Road in Overland. His older son, Jimmie Lee Green, bought out his siblings, Sherri and David.

Jimmie was like his father in that he liked saloon society, but he was unlike his dad on the domestic front. He met his true love in junior high. Linda was 13. He was 14. Jimmie got to Ritenour High School one year before her and they dated through high school. They married in June 1972, one week after Linda graduated.

Jimmie Lee Jr. was born in 1976. Jodi was born in 1978.

When Jimmie Lee Jr. was 13, his kidneys failed. Jimmie gave him one of his. Catastrophe averted. Jimmie Lee Jr. regained his health. He became a fine high school baseball pitcher.

Or maybe catastrophes are never averted. They're simply delayed. When Jimmie Lee Jr. was 30, he had gall bladder surgery and developed an infection. He died.

"He was a golden boy," said Linda.

By then, Jimmie was no longer a saloon keeper. The restaurant that owned the building on Woodson Road had decided to expand. Jimmie lost his space. He went into the karaoke business. He took his karaoke machine to saloons all over north St. Louis County and into St. Charles. He sometimes worked six nights a week. Eventually, he hired somebody so he could have more time off. It was a successful business.

A couple of years ago, he had a heart attack. He had open heart surgery to replace a valve. He also developed diabetes. His remaining kidney quit working and he went on dialysis. Then his replacement valve failed and he had more surgery.

Late last month, his second valve failed. Doctors told him he probably wouldn't survive another surgery, but without it, he had very little time remaining. Two weeks to six months, they said. Probably closer to two weeks.

Jimmie opted not to have surgery. He accepted the fact that he would soon die. He was a strong Christian, and he told Linda that he would soon see their son. He wanted to do a few things before he died.

One was to plan his funeral. He knew the music he wanted. He selected the song, "I Did It My Way."

Also, he wanted to be baptized. He and his family were members of the Garden Baptist Church on Midland Boulevard. He got his diagnosis on Thursday, Aug. 29, and that next Sunday, he was baptized.

Finally, he wanted to say goodbye to all his friends in the saloon society. A party was quickly planned for the next Thursday night at Houdini's, a bar on Lackland Road in Overland. The location made sense for a couple of reasons. First, it was one of his regular stops on his karaoke route, and Thursday night was his night there. Second, his sister, Sherri Erickson, tended bar at Houdini's. Who better to put out the word?

Jimmie wasn't feeling too well that day. Linda wasn't sure he should go out. Perhaps it would be better to stay home and spend the night with their daughter, Jodi Green-Wiley, and her kids, Malia, 12, and Ethan, 10.

But Jimmie wouldn't hear of it. The fact that he was feeling weak was all the more reason to say his goodbyes. Off they went to Houdini's. Jimmie was in a wheelchair.

The place was completely jammed. It was packed like nobody had ever seen. "We ran out of beer, " said Sherri. Jimmie sat next to the karaoke machine and greeted people. More than one person thought it was like being at his own wake, but a joyous Irish wake it was.

Toward midnight, good friend Norm Renner approached Jimmie to pay his respects. "I'm done, Norm. I'm done, " Jimmie said.

Shortly thereafter, Linda took Jimmie home. David, his brother, followed in his car. Jimmie lost consciousness on the way home. Linda stopped her car. David stopped his and came over to help. He and Linda were able to revive Jimmie. When they arrived at Jimmie and Linda's home in St. Ann, they went to get the wheelchair out of the car.

"No, I'll walk, " Jimmie said. And with Linda's help, he did. He walked into his living room and he sat in his chair. Then he died.

Sherri arrived a few minutes later. She called the bar to let the crowd know that Jimmie had died. The person who answered the phone had a hard time understanding her. The karaoke machine was going. It was playing, "I Did It My Way."

NOVEMBER 27, 2011

Missourah getting back to its roots

Missouri has finally seceded.

I think the credit belongs to state Sen. Jason Crowell of Cape Girardeau. People underestimate him. He got a lot of attention during his days in the House when he used to make flatulent sounds into his microphone when opponents were trying to talk. Sometimes he made siren sounds.

This kind of childish behavior led people to think of him strictly as a buffoon, but he has a serious side, as well.

He is serious about economics. He thinks we should become a "right to work" state. He was pushing the idea a year ago. He wanted it to be on the ballot in 2012.

I wrote about his efforts. I admitted I wasn't up to speed on economics. I wrote, "I don't spend enough time in the states Crowell wants to emulate — Alabama, Georgia, Mississippi, Arkansas and so on — to know how well they're doing."

What do all of those states have in common?

They're in the SEC. Along with Kentucky, Florida, South Carolina, Tennessee and Louisiana.

The Old South.

Is this where Missouri belongs?

That depends. Are you talking about Missouree or Missourah?

We are a state divided, and have been for more than 150 years. We can't get over the Civil War.

That's why the governor appoints the members of the St. Louis Police Board. In 1861, Confederate sympathizers in Jefferson City put control of the police under the governor for fear that the Union sympathizers would use the police against the rebel supporters.

In fact, earlier this month, one of my colleagues on the editorial page — a nest of Union sympathizers, by the way — wrote an editorial suggesting that a ballot initiative seeking to return control to the city should say, "Shall the state of Missouri declare that the Civil War is over?"

For many years, the University of Missouri struggled with this legacy. It belonged to a conference that included northern states like Colorado, Nebraska, Iowa and Kansas. Kansas! The hated rival from the days of the Civil War. The Jayhawkers. Unionists.

That rivalry is now over. Gone with the wind, you might say.

Missouri is with the Confederacy.

Sadly, not everybody has gotten the memo. Like the Boone County Sheriff's Department. It was a member of that department who recently gave football coach Gary Pinkel a ticket for DWI.

Maybe that happens in the Big 12. It does not happen in the SEC. You think Bear Bryant ever got a DWI? Certainly not in Alabama. SEC football coaches expect a little latitude. If you want to give somebody a ticket, give it to the basketball coach. This ain't the ACC.

Perhaps we're seeing a little pushback. Maybe somebody doesn't want to join the Confederacy. This is a Southern state, a red state, but there are blue dots. St. Louis, Kansas City, Columbia.

Columbia. That's Boone County, isn't it?

Maybe it's time the legislators take local control of the sheriff's department away from Boone County. If the Yankees in Boone County don't want to acknowledge we're in the SEC, the heck with them. But do you trust the governor with control?

Last I remember, Gov. Jay Nixon was openly pushing for the university to join the Big Ten.

That conference includes Illinois, Ohio, Wisconsin, Pennsylvania, Indiana, Iowa, Michigan and Minnesota.

Does that sound like a crowd Missouri would run with?

I think not.

Nixon does his best to hide his Democratic leanings, but a preference for the Big Ten is telling. Those are northern states, Union states, blue states.

Football coaches can get in trouble up there. Look at Jim Tressel of Ohio State.

Look at Joe Paterno of Penn State. A coach can lose his job for something other than losing football games. Is that what Mizzou wants?

Again, I think not.

I understand that some folks are sorry to see the old rivalries disappear. But this is a new time, the bright dawn of a new era.

In a way, it's as if the state has been given a do-over. Back in 1861, we teetered this way and that, and finally flopped over to the Union side. We've more or less stayed there for the last 150 years.

Now we're going to give the other side a try. We're going to join the states Crowell has been pushing us to emulate — Alabama, Louisiana, Mississippi and so forth.

It might seem strange for a university to change conferences only because of the football team, but that's the Yankee way of looking at things. In the SEC, we'd say that the football team is changing conferences and the university is tagging along.

Missourah is finally a happy place.

MARCH 17, 2013

Newspaper salesman at hospital gets a new set of wheels

The alarm goes off shortly after 4 a.m. and Jim Stoien prepares to go to the Barnes-Jewish Hospital complex for another day of work. After a simple breakfast, he heads toward the complex about a half-mile away. He walks with a sideways gait. His right arm is in a sling. With his left arm, he pushes a shopping cart. The city is just stirring to life.

Stoien sells newspapers. The carrier leaves about 100 for him. Stoien also loads his cart with free newspapers and magazines. These he gives away. Also, candy. He likes to give candy away.

He starts at the Siteman Cancer Center. He goes next to Children's Hospital, and then to Barnes-Jewish. He goes floor to floor, room to room. He has been doing this since 1981. He has more seniority than most official employees, and he has earned almost complete access. Everybody knows him.

"Hello, Jim, " people will say.

"Play ball. Play ball, " he responds.

He used to carry mementos of a past life. One was a report titled, "Post-Irradiation Effects of Photoreactivating Light and Caffeine on Cultured Marsupial Cells Exposed to Ultraviolet Light." He presented that report at a seminar in the spring of 1975. At the time, he was a 28-year-old National Science Foundation scholar working on a doctoral degree in microbiology at the University of Colorado.

If you looked at the report and asked if he wrote it, he would shrug and say, "Years ago. Years ago."

His mementos included a couple of columns I have written about him. In those columns, I mentioned that he was a popular student at McCluer High School. He was one of the 10 senior boys selected for the homecoming court in 1964. Then he went to the University of Missouri. After graduating, he did a hitch in the Army. He was an officer. He did a tour in Germany.

In the fall of 1975, he was riding his bicycle home from campus in Boulder, Colo. He was hit by a car. In those days, nobody wore helmets. He was in a coma for eight weeks. He did not speak for 4½ years. According to medical reports written about his recovery, the onset of speech was sudden and unexpected. He counted to 10. He said he wanted a beer. He laughed and laughed.

But the recovery was not complete. Jim communicates with a few well-worn phrases. "Play ball. Play ball, " is his favorite.

That is pretty much where the last column ended 13 years ago. Jim was cheerfully carrying on.

He's had ups and downs since then. His mother died several years ago. That was a blow. They used to play dominoes for hours every Saturday. With his mother gone, he started drinking more beer and letting his apartment go, which was a problem because Jim was something of a hoarder. Maybe because he'd lost so much, he wanted to hold on to what he had.

But then there was another miracle. With the encouragement of his siblings, he turned things around. He joined a 12-step program. He's been sober for more than three years. Every Wednesday, he plays dominoes with his sister, Dianne Ritter. He agreed to let a cleaning woman come in every other week.

Through it all, he continued selling papers.

A couple of weeks ago, he slipped as he was crossing the street. His cart got away from him. A car ran into it. Not only was the cart ruined, but Jim's papers were scattered and lost. Somebody at the hospital "borrowed" a cart from an area grocery store.

Dianna Harris, a nurse in the Barnes-Jewish discharge lounge, set out to get him a new cart. She called National Cart in St. Charles, and National agreed to give him a special lightweight model. Dianna and her colleagues, including Heather Meador, decorated the cart with Cardinals paraphernalia. They put a bicycle horn on the handle. They collected money from colleagues and bought candy for Jim to give away and coupons he could use in the hospital cafeteria. They gave him a baseball signed by Stan Musial.

Dianna called the Cardinals to see if Jim could get some kind of recognition on BJC Day at Busch Stadium. That is still up in the air, she said.

She also did her best to re-create his mementos. She bought a scrapbook and put photos of hospital employees and Cardinals in it. Through an Internet search, she managed to find the paper Jim presented in 1975.

Dianna, her colleagues and hospital officials presented the cart, the gifts and the scrapbook to Jim on Wednesday afternoon.

"Take me out to the ball game, " he said. "Take me out to the ball game."

SEPTEMBER 4, 2013

No one to name faces in photos

After my father died, I cleaned out the mobile home he and my mother had lived in. I wondered what artifacts to save. A clock perhaps? A throw rug? I opted for two coffee cups.

Also, a cardboard box filled with photos. I figured I would go through the photos when I had a chance. Years passed. Decades, really. My dad died before my son was born, and Jack is now 26.

I went though the photos this weekend.

There were a number of photos of my late sister and me when we were little. Photos of our dog, Sparky. These were snapshots – literally – of life in a working-class neighborhood of Chicago more than half a century ago. Full of myself, I decided these were historical and definitely worth keeping. Maybe not all of them, but many of them.

My parents were in plenty of the photos. I saved most of them.

There were photos of my grandmother, who was born in Belfast. She lived with us. She was an elfin figure, tiny and filled with the magic and prejudices of the old country. When I was in fifth grade, I told her I liked a girl in my class. My grandmother said, "She's a Catholic. That wouldn't work."

Also photos of her sister Sarah, who lived with us for a while until dementia set in. Back then, dementia was not a word. People just said somebody had gone crazy. My family stories are heavy with these two characters.

Perhaps my kids will tell their kids the stories. With that in mind, I saved some of the photos.

Then I got to the really old photographs. These were from the early years of the last century, from a time before working people had cameras. So they were studio shots in cardboard frames.

They were of much higher quality than the snapshots, and they spoke of a time when people got dressed up for baseball games, let alone a visit to a photographer. The people looked elegant.

But who were they?

I suspect a lot of us have photos like this in boxes in the basement. Essentially, they are photos of strangers.

Had I known of these photos, I could have asked my mother about them. She could have given the people names. Uncle Phil. Aunt Polly. Stories, too. My mother was a storyteller. The people in the photos could have come to life. Where they grew up, what they did, their foibles. They were, after all, real people.

The thought struck me that there is nobody now living who could identify these people. I have no aunts or uncles. I am not in touch with any cousins, so I doubt that anybody is interested in genealogy.

I also realized that I have never seen a photo of my dad's parents, Reginald and Gertrude. I know very little about them. They lived on the south side of Chicago. Reginald was an engineer for the Illinois Central Railroad, and he became disabled. I do not know how. But it was in the days before safety nets, so life was difficult.

During the Great Depression, my father had a chance to get a job, but the company required that he join the National Guard. Reginald forbade it. He was a railroad man, and he considered the National Guard to be strikebreakers. So my dad did not take the job, and the family struggled.

Was a young Reginald one of the people in the photos?

I have his railroad watch. I don't carry it, but I keep it in a drawer that I am into and out of every day. Now and then I notice it. Perhaps that means something. They say a person is really dead only when nobody alive ever thinks of them.

In the spirit of the railroad watch, when my son turned 21, I gave him my father's fedora. First, I took it to the Levine Hat Co. on Washington Avenue. Edward Levine, who is 79, is the patriarch of that business. He believes in hats. "I wouldn't take out the garbage without wearing a hat," he once told me. I asked if he could repair my father's fedora. He could. Actually, longtime manager James "Pete" Peterson could.

Was Reginald in one of photos? There is no way to know.

The same is true of Gertrude. Perhaps she is one of the women smiling into the camera. It would have been on a long-ago day in Chicago. An unusual day, out of the ordinary, going to a photo studio. I imagine a young woman, fussing, trying to look as good as possible. She would probably take the streetcar. Or maybe she walked. Probably more fussing once she got to the studio. Or maybe not. Maybe she was a serious young woman. I have no idea.

But whoever these people were, they posed and then they got on with their lives. Eventually, their photos ended up in my basement, where I looked at them this weekend, and thought, Who were these people?

MARCH 5, 2014

Our best fans don't need Cardinal Way

The news comes from Florida that the Cardinals have several more great young pitchers. As a Cubs fan, I can relate. The Cubs have had young phenoms, too. We had Dick Drott in 1957 and Kerry Wood in 1998. At that rate, we can expect another great young pitcher in 2039.

So, yes, I am jealous, but I am also happy for Cardinals fans. I really am. Many of my friends root for the Cardinals. But I would like to make one minor request. Could we stop this "Cardinal Way" stuff?

I picked up the paper the other day, and turned, as I usually do, to the Sports section. Ah, good. There was a column by my friend and colleague, Bernie Miklasz. Here was the headline: "Shortstop Peralta adjusting quickly to Cardinal Way."

I was hoping we were done with that. I don't remember hearing much about the Cardinal Way until last postseason. The series against the Los Angeles Dodgers was framed as a morality play. The Dodgers were the bad guys, the show-offs. The Cardinals were the good guys who believed in the Cardinal Way.

They were a bunch of Luke Skywalkers playing baseball. May the Way be with you.

Some of it was hard for me to understand. For instance, when a Dodger hit a double and stood on second base pounding his chest, it was because he was an egotistical show-off. When a Cardinal hit a double and stood on second base pounding his chest, it was because he was happy for his team. He was pounding his chest because he believed in the Cardinal Way.

In truth, I couldn't tell the difference.

During that series, a strange thing happened. People around the country began to dislike the Cardinals. I remember reading stories in which the writers said it was a compliment. And yes, in a way it was. When I was a kid, many people disliked the Yankees. That's because they won so much. That certainly explained the resentment that some people felt toward the Cardinals.

But I suspect some of it had to do with the Cardinal Way.

It's like that "Best Fans in Baseball" stuff. When I arrived here in 1980, St. Louisans weren't calling themselves the best fans in baseball. They seemed to consider themselves good fans, very good fans, the equal to any fans in the country. As good as fans in Detroit. As good as fans in Chicago. As good as fans in Pittsburgh. Better than fans in Philadelphia. (They boo too much.) But not the best fans.

Of course, St. Louis was a Midwestern city back then. Midwesterners are understated. Over the years, Missouri has slid down the map and taken St. Louis with it. We're Southerners now. Southerners aren't understated.

After disposing of the Dodgers, the Cardinals played Boston in the World Series. What an insufferable World Series that was. The Cardinal Way versus Boston Strong. Oh, how I longed for the days when baseball games weren't so fraught with meaning. If you liked team-oriented, moral, holistic people, you had to root for the Cardinal Way. But if you wanted to stand with the heroic people who persevered through the terrorist bombing of the Boston Marathon, you had to root for Boston Strong.

With the World Series long behind us, I was hoping this would be a new season. More baseball, less moralizing. There was reason to be optimistic. The Cardinals made a big splash in the offseason by signing Jhonny Peralta to a megabucks contract despite the fact that he was caught up in the Biogenesis scandal a year ago and suspended for 50 games.

Initially, he proclaimed his innocence. "I have never used performance-enhancing drugs. Period. Anybody who says otherwise is lying." Then he accepted his suspension.

I have nothing against players who use performance-enhancing drugs. The difference between being a pretty good baseball player and a very good baseball player is measured in millions.

But is it the morally upright thing to do? Hardly.

Then Carlos Martinez had that embarrassing business with links to porn sites on his Twitter account. I have nothing against anybody who looks at pornography, but I am suspicious of people with Twitter accounts. Why does that person think the rest of the world cares what he thinks? There is no "i" in team, but there is definitely an "i" in Twitter.

Is that the Cardinal Way? Hardly.

By the way, Bernie ended his story about Peralta with this line: "Getting comfortable with his new team, Peralta is quickly learning the way. The Cardinal Way."

I am imploring the Best Fans in Baseball: Please, stop.

FEBRUARY 23, 2014

Paying it forward with donor drives

On a Saturday last September, Be the Match Foundation sponsored a 5-kilometer walk and run in Creve Coeur Park to promote donor awareness. The foundation is an international bone marrow registry, and it coordinates marrow and stem cell transplants that are used to treat blood disorders.

Mark Pearl was at the event. Two of his three kids were born with a rare blood disorder called Fanconi anemia. Alexandra was diagnosed on Christmas Day 2000. She was 5. Her younger brother, Matthew, was diagnosed shortly thereafter. A marrow donor in Sweden was quickly found for Alexandra, but no matches were found for Matthew.

Mark and his wife, Diane, began organizing donor drives. It's easy to register as a donor. A couple of swabs on the inside of a cheek to collect DNA is all that is required. At their first drive in February 2001, they registered more than 4,000 potential donors. No matches. Over the next five and a half years, they organized more than 1,000 drives and registered more than 100,000 potential donors.

A donor was eventually found in North Carolina. As is almost always the case, the donor registered at someone else's drive. Matthew received his transplant in 2006.

He and his sister are fine.

Also at the event in Creve Coeur was Brian Jakubeck. He did not know Mark, but he had registered as a potential donor at one of the drives the Pearls had organized for Matthew. One of the last drives, actually.

How did that happen? Mark has season tickets for the Rams and sits next to Ted Cassimatis, who is a college friend of Brian's brother. So as the Pearls reached out well beyond their own circle of friends, Ted sent out a mass email to his friends, and that email reached Brian. He and his wife, Kathy, registered as potential donors at a drive in May 2006.

Sometime later, Brian heard the good news from Ted that a donor had been found for his friend's son.

Several years passed. In August 2012, Brian heard from Be the Match. He appeared to be a match. Would he agree to have some blood samples taken to confirm that he was a match? Sure, he said.

The results were positive. He was a match. He had more tests shortly before Christmas, and in January of last year, he went to St. Louis University Hospital and gave his stem cells. This was done in a process called apheresis. It is similar to giving plasma or platelets. The blood goes through an IV, passes through a machine that collects the stem cells, and then is returned through another IV. It's painless, but takes about six hours.

As is the custom, Brian was not given the name or location of his recipient. Just the recipient's age, sex and disease. If both donor and recipient want to exchange information, the exchange can be made one year after the transplant.

Also at the walk and run was Jeff Haertling. He registered as a donor in 2007 when a friend's daughter was looking for a match. Sadly, a match was not found, and she died of leukemia. But a couple of years later, he was a match for a 16-year-old girl in the state of Washington who was fighting a blood cancer. She received Jeff's stem cells and survived. He now considers her part of his family, and he is part of hers.

Haertling does a lot of volunteer work for Be the Match.

Dennis Gittemeier was also at the event. He was there as a recipient. He lives in St. Charles. A couple of years ago, he started feeling tired. Beyond tired, really. He went to the doctor. He was diagnosed with myelodysplasia, a rare blood disorder curable only by a bone marrow transplant.

He had a donor drive. Jeff attended. The two talked. Jeff explained that people don't find a match at their own drive. It's more a thing of paying it forward. Maybe somebody from your drive will be a match for somebody else. That's the way it works.

Dennis got a match almost immediately. He had his transplant a year ago last month. He said he definitely wanted to meet his donor when the year was up.

Last month, the year was up. Dennis was hoping his donor came from someplace warm. Meanwhile in south St. Louis County, Brian was waiting to learn the identity of his recipient. He was hoping his recipient came from someplace warm. Both men were willing to travel.

South County, meet St. Charles.

They met last weekend at a trivia night to benefit Be The Match. They laughed when they realized they'd been at the same event in September. Probably just a few yards apart.

They got together with Jeff and Mark on Wednesday in Soulard. Mark said he thought the drives for his son resulted in at least 800 matches. Maybe somebody from Dennis' drive will be a match for somebody, Jeff said, and everybody seemed to agree that this is a story without an ending.

FEBRUARY 12, 1990

Retired cops want justice to be done

Gregory Sullivan was 9 years old when his father, a city cop, was killed in the line of duty.

That happened 53 years ago. In the intervening years, Sullivan grew up, became a cop himself, and retired. He was a "company man." The department was his family. So it has to feel a little strange to be leading a gang of dissidents.

But that's just what Sullivan is doing. He's the unofficial head of the "Committee of Unrefunded Retired St. Louis Police Officers."

More than two-thirds of the fellows the committee represents are past the age of 70. Sullivan, at 62, is one of the youngest.

To understand their cause, you have to understand a basic fact about the police pension plan.

A cop contributes 8 percent of his pay to the retirement fund. The city matches that contribution. When a cop retires, he receives, in a lump sum, the amount of money that he has paid into the fund.

That is, of course, in addition to his pension, the size of which is based on a formula involving salary and time of service.

If a person has paid $22,000 into the fund, he gets a check for $22,000.

It's been that way since September 1981.

Sullivan's committee is made up of the guys who retired before that date.

They'd like to get their money back.

Earlier this week, a group of the retirees got together for coffee. They spent part of the time chatting about the old days.

They talked about the way it was 50 years ago when most of them first joined the force. They talked about walking a beat, using a call box to check in with the station every hour. There were no portable radios, no walkie-talkies.

But we controlled those streets, one said, and the others quickly agreed. As you might expect, they had some fine stories.

What an unlikely group of dissidents, I thought to myself.

They were 79, 78, 75, 74 and 69. And Sullivan, the baby, at 62.

Then the talk turned to the pension fund.

Here are the hard facts. The police pension fund currently has assets of $359 million. There are about 400 fellows who retired before 1981. The number, of course, decreases every year.

Because salaries were so much lower in the old days, the older retirees put in a lot less money than the officers who are contributing today.

The average contribution for the older guys is about $10,000. If the fund were to pay them off tomorrow, the total payout would be about $4 million.

The pension fund would still have $355 million in assets, and everybody who had contributed would have his money back.

Here's the human side of the equation. Many of the older guys were on the force when secondary employment was not allowed. A lot of these fellows stayed in the department until they were 65. Consequently, they did not qualify for Social Security.

In fact, most of the older retirees who are getting Social Security are getting the minimum. They qualified only because they served in the military during World War II.

Plus, they're members of a generation in which the husband worked, and the wife stayed home. So their spouses aren't getting Social Security.

Throw in the fact that salaries were low during their working days — and pensions are based on salaries — and you can see that some of these older guys are not at all well off. There are retired city cops trying to make it on less than $500 a month.

Oh, would a $10,000 check come in handy!

"I'd cash mine, take my shoes off, throw the money on the floor and just spend hours walking around in it," said one of the guys.

Everybody laughed, but to these fellows, some of whom have a desperate need for money, the unrefunded money is hardly a laughing matter.

They feel betrayed.

They think that today's cops think only of themselves, and don't want to be bothered with the cops of yesteryear. They think that the Police Veterans Association is unconcerned because most of the retirees who belong to that organization have retired since 1981.

The older guys have been to the Legislature, and in 1984, the Legislature passed a bill that would allow the pension fund to draw up a program in which the older guys could get their contributions back.

But nothing has come of that. No program has been devised.

At the pension fund meeting in January, Sullivan appeared in front of the board of trustees, and asked that a member, any member, make a motion to develop a program to pay the pre-1981 retirees their contributions.

He got no takers.

After talking with Sullivan and his friends, I called Lt. Manuel Delgado, one of the police department representatives on the pension board. I know Delgado, and he is not a man without compassion.

He said he sympathized with the older guys.

"You know, another benefit a lot of them don't get is the cost of living increase. If they retired before 1975, they don't get that. That's unfair, too, but that's the law."

Well, as long as the law says the pension fund can pay these guys the money they put in, and as long as everybody else gets back the money they put in, why not do it? After all, when you're talking about a pension fund of $359 million, $4 million doesn't seem like much.

"I know it doesn't sound like much, but I'm told that if we pulled out four and a half million, the fund would be fiscally unsound. This is all very complicated," Delgado said.

Undoubtedly, it is. At least in a financial sense.

But as far as fairness goes, it doesn't seem complicated at all.

Besides, I can just see a 79-year-old man taking off his shoes, and wading through a sea of twenties.

NOVEMBER 10, 2013

Saving strays comes with no guarantees

Gregory Berin goes to Stray Rescue several times a week and walks whatever dog they give him. On a recent night, it was a bulldog-terrier mix named Meathead.

"I know how they feel being penned up," Berin said.

Berin is 51. He got out of prison in August. He'd been penned up for 13 years. That was just his last stretch. He's been to prison a total of five times. His first sentence began in July 1983. In the 30 years since, he has been in and out, mostly in. He has been free for a total of 37 months. Prison officials refer to such a history as a life sentence on the installment plan.

Not surprisingly, Berin said he is done with prison. He said he is a changed man.

He used to be a thief. Maybe the worst kind of a thief. He stole from people he knew, people who trusted him. What's more, he didn't have to steal. At least not at first. He stole for the thrill of it. Later, when his criminal record made it difficult to get a job, there were times when he stole to pay bills. That is how he tells the story.

He said he has finally turned a corner in his life. He took all the right rehabilitative courses in prison. He said he has his mind right for the first time in years. Mainly, though, he has the support of Project COPE, a nonprofit organization that offers a variety of services to help men and women when they get out of prison.

In a sense, it's a Stray Rescue for people.

Berin will be a challenge. On the night he took Meathead for a walk, he said all the right things. He took responsibility for all the bad things he has done in the past.

On the other hand, part of being a thief is being a con man. In his most infamous theft, he victimized a young woman who had fallen in love with him. According to a made-for-television movie, he proposed to her before stealing her grandmother's jewelry and then her own. According to the movie, she was a private detective who became suspicious and then helped the police arrest the man whom she had thought of as Prince Charming.

Berin told me the parts about the thievery were accurate. He said he stole jewelry from her and her grandmother. He said the romance angle was overdone. I was unable to reach the woman.

Crime was not part of Berin's upbringing, but jewelry was. He said his parents owned a jewelry store across Clayton Road from Plaza Frontenac. He had a normal, happy childhood and graduated from Parkway Central in 1982. He said that was about the time he started stealing. If he didn't need the money, why did he do it?

"Originally, it was a thrill," he said. "An impulse. Something comes over you, and instead of thinking about it, you just do it."

He said he has a twin brother and a sister. Neither has been in trouble.

When a person gets in trouble over and over, he burns a lot of bridges. When Berin was released from prison in August, nobody came to pick him up. He took a Greyhound bus to St. Louis.

Thanks to Project COPE, he had a place to live. Also, a support team. Counseling, too.

"I'm not walking a tightrope without a net below me, anymore, " he said.

He's found a part-time job. He's looking for full-time work. He's supposed to transition out of his current apartment in a few months. Typically, landlords want first and last month rent and a security deposit.

Project COPE has a history of success. It has been around since 1984, and it claims a success rate of 86 percent. It sends volunteers into prison to screen potential clients. Actually, it calls the newly released men and women "partners."

So Berin was screened and then selected. Project COPE has a strong religious slant. Churches are involved. The people who volunteer believe in redemption.

I thought about that as I watched Berin and Meathead stroll along the streets near Stray Rescue, which is on Pine Street just east of Jefferson Avenue. It was an early evening, chilly, and the end of rush hour traffic was zipping past. Nobody paid much attention to the man and the dog. Two strays, almost invisible. The dog completely without guile, the man a question mark. I'm sure it's possible for a con man to reform, but how can you tell?

The next day, I stopped at Stray Rescue to learn more about Meathead. Where had he been picked up? How long had he been at the shelter?

A worker told me such information is confidential.

Berin told me he's walked Meathead before. So maybe he'll get him again. If you happen to be driving some late afternoon or early evening in the western part of downtown, and you see a guy about 50 walking a bulldog-terrier mix, give them a wave. Or say a prayer. They both need some luck.

DECEMBER 15, 2008

Scent of pine wafts family back to time of love, wholeness

Many, many years ago, in a city far to our north, there lived a family with seven children.

Marjorie was the oldest. If you had to describe the family's economic situation, you would call it middle class. Maybe even lower middle class. But whatever it was, it was comfortable and secure. At least it seemed so to the children.

Truth is, there were storm clouds just over the horizon. The most personal had to do with the health of the father. As a child, he had suffered from rheumatic fever. The illness had left him with a weakened heart.

But the children were unaware of their father's health problem. More precisely, they were unaware of its implications. The fact that their father was not a robust man – you and I might call him sickly – was just that, a fact. Neither good nor bad. Just a fact.

Oddly enough, the children recall their father as a man of extraordinary strength. His strength was spiritual rather than physical. He was a man of great religious faith. It was not the type of faith that manifests itself in self-righteousness. His God was a loving God.

The house and the family were filled with love.

Because of the father's religious faith, the holiday season was not festive. The father believed in Advent. That is, the weeks before Christmas were spent in quiet contemplation. As a true Christian, he was preparing himself for the celebration of the birth of Jesus.

The children, on the other hand, were waiting for Christmas Eve.

They knew that their father had already bought a Christmas tree and had stored it in the garage. They knew that at precisely 6:30 on Christmas Eve, their parents would send them upstairs to bed. Then their parents would bring in the Christmas tree, decorate it and put the presents underneath it.

Sometime after 11, their parents would leave the house to go to midnight Mass.

Technically, of course, their father — their devout father! — was rushing the end of Advent by a few hours. But as I've said, his God was a loving God and therefore understood that seven children would wake up early on Christmas morning and expect to find a well-decorated Christmas tree.

At any rate, there was a magical moment to all of this.

And that magical moment came when the children had been sent upstairs and their father brought the tree in from the garage.

When the tree was brought from the cold garage into the warm house, an overpowering scent of pine wafted upstairs. It filled the nostrils of the children. For them, this sudden smell of pine meant Christmas.

The oldest boy was always detailed to hide near the top of the stairs and to report to the rest of the children when their parents had left for church.

Then the children would tumble down the stairs, gaze in wonderment at the tree and the presents and finally rush upstairs as their parents returned from church.

And so it went, year after year, even as the storm clouds gathered over the horizon.

The father's heart grew ever weaker. On a grander scale, an unemployed house painter was gaining a following in Germany.

Eventually, the storms came. The father died at the age of 47, while the youngest children were still children. The oldest son, the boy who had once hid near the top of the stairs, was killed in World War II.

On his very last bombing mission — he was scheduled to come home after the flight — his plane was hit and he bailed out over the English Channel. His body was never recovered.

By this time, Marjorie was a Dominican nun. Eventually, three of her four sisters joined her in the order.

Marjorie is now 70 years old. She is happy, and at peace, but every year as Christmas approaches, she follows the same ritual.

First, she buys a small tree. But that is not enough. So then she buys pine boughs and scatters them around her small apartment. But that is not enough.

Finally, then, she buys an aerosol can of pine scent. She sprays it, almost madly, around the apartment. She breathes in the odor.

For an instant, as the scent of pine overwhelms her, she catapults back in time.

One of her younger sisters, a nun here in St. Louis, is a friend of mine. She lovingly kids Marjorie about the ritual.

But also, she understands.

That sudden rush of pine scent can throw her, too, back to a simpler time when the family was whole and Christmas had a magic that went beyond even religion.

Enjoy what you have this holiday season, my friend tells me, and I pass the message on to you on this Christmas Eve.

If you're blessed enough to be surrounded by love, rejoice.

Update: Marjorie is now 85. She still seeks the scent of pine at Christmas. My friend, her sister, is also still active. "Dominican nuns don't retire," Sister Joan Delaplane told me. "We just redirect our energies." Her energies are presently directed at retreat work.

FEBRUARY 19, 1997

Sign of a random act of kindness: 'Take my truck'

Last summer, a friend and I motored a small boat up the Illinois River to Chicago, and then followed the shoreline of the big lake all the way up into northern Michigan.

We had many fine adventures along the way, but the incident that we always talk about when we relive the trip was not an adventure at all. It was a 10-minute drive in a pickup. We had arrived in the small Illinois River town of Havana. We pulled close to the shore. I jumped on to the bank – OK, I landed, as always, in the mud near the bank – and I tied the boat to a tree. My friend threw me our empty gasoline cans, and then joined me on the shore.

We started into town, looking for the closest gas station.

It turned out to be about a mile away. Well, fine. We figured we'd hoof to the gas station, fill up our five-gallon cans, and then cadge a ride back to our boat. Those cans are heavy when they're full. When you travel on a river, you can almost always count on the kindness of strangers.

At any rate, we began hoofing along the main drag, heading toward the distant gas station. We walked past three construction workers, who were taking their lunch break.

"You fellows coming from the river?" one of them asked us.

"You bet. Gotta gas up," my friend said.

We had only gone a few feet past them when one of them hollered. We stopped and looked back.

"Take my truck," he said. Then he pointed to the truck at the curb and tossed us the keys.

The man didn't even know our names.

So we did take the man's truck. We got our gasoline and drove it back to our boat. When we returned the truck, we talked for a few minutes with its owner.

His name is Bill Parsley, and he was the sort of friendly, open man who would, well, tell a couple of strangers to take his truck.

Admittedly, Havana seems like the kind of place where people don't lock their doors, and my friend and I are products of places where suspicion is the watchword, so maybe you'd expect guys like us to be astounded at old-fashioned, small-town attitudes.

Take my truck.

It became like a mantra to us. It represented the world as it should be.

About 10 days ago, my friend and his teen-age son were driving along Clayton Road near the Galleria. They came upon a van barely moving. And no wonder. Something, maybe the exhaust system, was dragging along the ground. Sparks were flying.

My friend stopped to help. There was a young woman driving and she had a baby in a car seat. With my friend following, she managed to get the car to a gas station.

My friend asked where she was headed. She said she was going to the Galleria to pick up her husband and their son.

"I'll take you," said my friend.

The young woman, being a city sort, was wary, but the presence of my friend's son probably seemed reassuring. Plus, she had to get to the Galleria. So she grabbed her baby and climbed into my friend's car.

He is, I should add, a good-deed doer, city fellow or not.

At the Galleria, the woman's husband and young son were waiting. The husband, like his wife before him, seemed suspicious. Why was my friend going to this much trouble for strangers?

"Your van is at a gas station," my friend said. "They're seeing if they can get it fixed tonight."

He then drove the family to the gas station. Bad news was waiting. The mechanic couldn't get the van fixed until morning.

So the husband thanked my friend, and said he'd call a taxi to get his family back to their home in St. Charles.

My friend lives near the gas station.

"Take my car," he said. He handed the man his keys.

The man was taken aback.

"Do you even know my name?" he asked.

"Actually, I don't," said my friend. "I'll show you where I live. Just bring the car back tomorrow."

After a few protestations — waved off by my friend — the family climbed into the car and away they went.

"Dad, how could you do this?" asked my friend's son.

Less than an hour later, the man returned my friend's car. The man's wife had followed him in the family's other car.

"I'm an architect, and if you ever need any architectural work, please call me," said the man.

As my friend watched the man and his wife drive away, he felt good. If only for a moment, he had brought the old-fashioned, small-town ways to the big city. He turned to his wife, who, of course, knows the river stories by heart.

"I just paid Bill Parsley back," my friend said.

JULY 8, 2009

St. Louis is truly something special

There is something magical about living in St. Louis and going to the Muny in Forest Park to see "Meet Me in St. Louis."

Maybe if I lived in Tulsa, I'd be a big fan of "Oklahoma," but I don't think so. "Oklahoma" is a wonderful musical, but it doesn't speak to the people of Oklahoma today. It's about a time that is long gone.

That is not the case with "Meet Me in St. Louis." That play speaks to the people of St. Louis. It shouts to us. I'm thinking of one line in particular, and I'll get to that line in a minute, but first I want to say that I do not intend to encroach upon the territory of my friend and colleague Judy Newmark, whose review of this production appears on Page A15. This column is not intended as a review, and I will not be saying that this actor did well, and this actor did not, although I will have to say that two actors were miscast, but that, too, I will put aside for a moment.

I trust there is no need to review the plot. The Smiths live in St. Louis in the days before the World's Fair of 1904. Mr. Smith is offered a promotion that would take him to New York. He tells the family, and they get upset. They don't want to leave St. Louis.

That cuts to the quick, doesn't it? You know our history. Back when the country was founded, the successful people had no reason to leave the East Coast. The less successful pushed west. This clump of unsuccessful people reached St. Louis. The adventurous ones pushed on. The slackers stayed here. Much later, we built the Gateway Arch to honor the people who had the gumption to keep going. We are the only city in the world that has a memorial to honor those who left.

So this whole thing about leaving and not leaving is in our DNA.

Although our city's founders were slackers, they did do a couple of things right. Foremost among these things is the Muny. It is the largest outdoor theater in the country. It is a wonderful venue, and every few years, it presents "Meet Me in St. Louis."

I am not one to tell people what to do, but there are two things that every St. Louisan ought to do – catch Chuck Berry at his monthly show at Blueberry Hill in the Delmar Loop, and see a production of "Meet Me in St. Louis" at the Muny.

This year's production opened Monday and will run through Saturday.

I've seen it before, so I know how it turns out, but still, when the father relented and decided not to take the promotion, I almost cried for joy. And then he shouted the line that spoke to us all. "We'll stay here until we all rot!" he shouted.

"Amen! Amen!" is the way people in church might have responded, but theatergoers are a more refined crowd, and we merely murmured our approval. "Yes, we will stay here until we all rot," we whispered to each other. Haven't we all made that decision? Isn't it good to see it validated on stage?

I mentioned that two actors were miscast. One was Stephen Bogardus, who played the father and shouted the line that electrified us all. He did a nice job as the father, but I saw him after the show, and he was much too young to be the father. The father should be somebody about my age. Aren't there any mature actors available? Then I caught a glimpse of Lewis Stadlen, who played the grandfather. No way should he be younger than me!

Admittedly, I have reached the age where if I go out to hear a band, I seldom know a member of the band, but I often know the parents of a member of the band.

So it was with this production.

One of the members of the ensemble was Jordan Newmark. Her mother is my aforementioned colleague. I don't mean to embarrass Jordan, but let me quote from a story her mother wrote years ago about the morning after Jordan's birth when the pediatrician came into the room. – "So, I asked. 'Is she perfect?' 'Well,' said the pediatrician. Imagine a huge black pit. Imagine hurtling down it, with nothing to break your fall and no bottom in sight."

There was a problem with Jordan's heart. Dr. Tony Hernandez, a pediatric cardiologist, successfully performed the delicate operation to repair the heart. Several years later, Jordan was the St. Louis Heart Association's Heart Child, and her mother wrote the story quoted above. By that time, Hernandez was dead. He died of a heart attack. He was 58.

Jordan went on to the University of Michigan, and has begun a career in theater.

I thought about that, and then of course I thought about my own kids, and how good life has been for us in St. Louis, and as I do every time I see this play, I started to cry.

"Meet Me at St. Louis" at the Muny. It's something special.

JULY 24, 2006

Storm stirs up north vs. south power struggle on my street

We are a region divided. Some of us have power and some don't. Neighborhoods are divided in the same fashion. Even streets.

My street, for instance. Those of us on the south side have power. We were out for a couple of hours Wednesday night. Very quickly, our power was restored. The people on the north side of the street have been without power since the storm struck.

At first, it was fun. I would walk on to my porch and I'd be wearing a sweater. "It's cold inside," I'd yell to my neighbors across the street. They were sure to be outside, by the way. The heat had made the inside of their homes unbearable. They had pulled furniture out on to their porches or in their yards, and they sat there sullenly, the have-nots staring across at the haves. They could see the lights on in our houses, the television lights flickering. They could hear the steady hum of our air conditioners.

"Any extra blankets?" I'd yell at them. "I like to crank the A.C. up on these hot nights, and the rest of the family complains."

The first night, some of my neighbors seemed to chuckle. By the second night, they didn't respond. Their moods had become as dark as their side of the street.

One of them approached me one evening and asked for ice. He said the stores were sold out.

"I'd love to help," I said, "but if I give you any, I'd have to give some to everybody. Then what happens if my power goes out? I'd be caught short. Sorry."

He shook his head and returned to his side of the street.

My wife developed a form of survivor's guilt. She didn't enjoy sitting on our porch with our porch light blazing. Although we couldn't see our neighbors across the street, we could feel their eyes. They were watching us. I felt like part of the oligarchy in a Third World country.

Sometimes neighbors from the south side of the street – the good side of the street – would come by and we'd laugh and chat. Always, though, we were aware of the people on the other side of the street staring at us out of the darkness.

"I like to think we'd be a little more gracious if this were reversed," I said to one of my neighbors. "I can just feel the resentment from those people on the north side. I like to think we'd be better sports about it. I can tell you that I wouldn't constantly be asking for ice or cold beverages. That gets old in a hurry."

My wife had a different attitude. She wanted to give ice away. She wanted to invite people over. Maybe they could even spend the night. We were just lucky, she said, and we should be willing to share our luck.

"Luck has nothing to do with this," I said. "We pay our bills promptly, and I suspect that's why AmerenUE has treated us well. I wouldn't be surprised if some of those people on the north side are behind on their bills. That probably explains it."

Actually, I had just thought of that, but I liked the sound of it. I repeated the theory to several of my neighbors from our side of the street, the good side, the side that pays its bills promptly.

"You think that's it?" one asked me.

"I'm quite sure of it," I said. "I doubt that Ameren wants to go public with this, but I don't believe luck plays much of a role in who has power and who doesn't."

That put a different spin on the resentment we were feeling from the north. Why were they blaming us for their own shortcomings? They had a lot of nerve. If nerve were electricity, their lights would be blazing.

Still, I've tried not to say much. Oh, I've speculated aloud to some of my south side neighbors about which of our north side neighbors are behind on their bills. "It's often the ones you wouldn't expect. Maybe the ones with the fanciest cars." But mostly, I've said nothing.

Have I resented the resentment from the north? Yes. It's made me uncomfortable, but I bear it in silence. After all, everyone will have power soon enough, and the region and the neighborhoods will come together again.

OCTOBER 6, 2010

Thoughts underlying a manager's quandary

While the St. Louis region holds its collective breath, Tony La Hamlet is driving across the country, struggling with the question that always torments him this time of year: to manage or not to manage.

That might be the question for him, but it would not be a vexing question for most of us. If you don't like your job and you can afford to quit, you quit. If you like your job or can't afford to quit, you keep going.

And really, what's not to like about managing a baseball team? You travel around the country, staying in the best hotels and eating at the finest restaurants. You have a pitching coach to help with your pitchers, and a hitting coach to help with your hitters. You walk around the field before the games and you sit in the dugout during the games. Plus, you have the winters off.

Not a bad gig, and in La Hamlet's case, somebody pays him $3 million a year to do it. What's not to like about that?

Nevertheless, this public show of angst has become a yearly tradition. Just as the swallows return to Capistrano, La Hamlet wrestles with his demons.

But the cross-country drive introduces a new element. Shakespeare meets American road trip.

Four years ago, I made the drive from St. Louis to the East Bay. I took the northern route with stops at Mount Rushmore and Little Bighorn.

I like to think La Hamlet is on that route. I imagine him cruising through the night on a lonely highway in northern Iowa. He is scowling, wearing dark glasses and pondering the future. There is no place like a desolate road in northern Iowa for soul-searching.

He drives through the night and stops at a gas station in South Dakota. He waits, impatiently, for an attendant to come fill his tank, and then realizes, "Oh, self-service. They're all self-service these days, aren't they?" It's moments like this that make a 66-year-old wonder if time has passed him by. I mean, this is something Joe

Torre might do. Or Bobby Cox. But wait. Doesn't La Hamlet have rock 'n' roll playing on CD? You're darned right he does. Some early Beatles, in fact. Something hip.

He adjusts his sunglasses and walks inside to pay for his gas and get a snack. He's humming "I Want to Hold Your Hand." He waits for the attendant to recognize him. Doesn't happen. He takes his sunglasses off. Changes the tune to "Take Me Out to the Ballgame." Still no reaction.

Is this good? Is this bad? On one hand, it's nice, at least for a moment, to be anonymous. On the other hand, he's Tony La Hamlet, the third-winningest manager in baseball history. He's friends with Bobby Knight and Bill Parcells. He is a national celebrity, and this idiot in the gas station doesn't have a clue. Probably some college kid studying journalism. A future sportswriter. In disgust, La Hamlet stalks back to his car.

He stops at Mount Rushmore for lunch. For no good reason, the Arch pops into his mind. "Maybe I should have visited it during my 15 years in St. Louis," he thinks. Then he wonders about the way he phrased that thought. Did he just put St. Louis in the past tense? Does that mean something?

He stares up at the faces on the mountain, and he feels unappreciated. How many games did any of those guys win? None. How many double-switches did they do? None. Yet there they are, their faces carved into stone, and here he is, only 125 games behind John McGraw, and he's sitting in the cafeteria.

Unnoticed, by the way. Even the Cardinals cap he has started wearing doesn't seem to have tipped anybody off as to his identity. Maybe if he managed one more year, got into one more World Series, maybe then everybody would recognize him. That gives him something to think about as he heads down the road to Little Bighorn.

He joins a tour at the battlefield. A ranger leads the group to the crest of a hill with a view of the Little Bighorn River. "This is where we think George Custer was when he first saw the Sioux encampment," the ranger says. "Obviously, we have no real way of knowing."

La Hamlet has always admired Custer. He considers him an unorthodox leader, the sort of man who would bat the pitcher eighth. He is almost overcome with emotion as he looks down toward the river.

He is now wearing his Cardinals cap and his Cardinals jacket — La Hamlet stitched on the back — but nobody seems to notice.

That no longer bothers him. One more World Series would take care of that. But what about his family, what about the stray dogs of Contra Costa County?

So he's back in the car, heading west. He's listening to rock 'n' roll again — the Turtles this time. And pondering: To manage or not to manage; that is the question.

Meanwhile, Cardinal Nation waits to exhale.

JANUARY 7, 2013

Time for honesty in gun debate

I have three predictions for the new year. First, there will be at least one horrific shooting with multiple victims. Second, an outraged citizenry will demand we do something. Third, no one will admit there is nothing we can do.

These shootings have become part of our lives. Sometimes at businesses, sometimes at schools, sometimes at churches, sometimes at restaurants. No place is safe. Twenty-one people were killed at a McDonald's restaurant in California. Twenty-three at a cafeteria in Texas. Thirteen at an Army base in Texas. Twelve at a temple in Wisconsin. On and on and on it goes.

A friend of mine recently went to see a movie. The theater darkened, and a man walked to the front. My friend, and probably most of the other people in the theater, experienced a moment of terror. Aurora, Colorado. Twelve killed. Then the man said he was the projectionist. He had some statement to make about cellphones.

I think the theater was irresponsible to have the projectionist do this. Somebody could have shot him.

There was a time when nobody would have thought about shooting the projectionist. A reader sent me a photo of a high school rifle team from the 1950s. She wrote, "You're probably too young to remember this, but kids used to keep rifles in their lockers."

I am not too young to remember that. My brother-in-law was on the rifle team. He went to a public high school in Chicago. He stored his rifle in his locker, too. Sometimes he took it home. On those days, he'd walk down the hall carrying his rifle. In the morning, he'd carry it back into school.

Of course, this was years before Columbine.

The Columbine shooting is interesting in two regards. One of the shooters had a TEC-9. He had three magazines for that weapon. One carried 52 rounds, one 32 rounds and one 28 rounds. The weapon he carried was banned at the time.

What good did the ban do?

The second interesting aspect is that an armed deputy was assigned to the school. He even got into a firefight with one of the shooters. It was after this shootout — and perhaps because of it — that the two killers went into the library, which is where they did most of their killing.

So much for the notion that the only thing that stops a bad guy with a gun is a good guy with a gun. Think about a fire-fight in a hallway if the bad guy has a rifle and the good guy has a sidearm. Who has the advantage?

I am not against armed guards at schools, and I am not against banning assault weapons, but I am against pretending that either would do much good.

One of the most horrific shootings in our area occurred in Kirkwood in 2008, when Charles Lee Thornton killed five people at City Hall. A sixth died later. Two of the victims were police officers. One was killed in the parking lot and the second was killed in City Hall.

If a shooter has the benefit of surprise, it doesn't matter if there is an armed guard.

Banning weapons won't do much good, either. There are so many of these weapons out there already that it would be easy for a person to get one. In fact, the more we talk about bans, the more we drive sales. It's the same thing with high-capacity magazines.

Truth is, a ban would be only symbolic.

An even worse idea is to ban their purchase and also make it illegal to own the existing ones. How would that work? It's almost like the debate about immigration. What do we do with millions of people who are living here illegally? Door-to-door searches? Ask them to self-deport?

We are not going to go door to door looking for assault rifles. We would not have much luck with a buyback program. I remember the first gun buyback program we had here in 1991. A child had been killed, and we wanted to do something. Just enough people turned in old and broken guns that we could melt them down and build a statue of the child.

Besides, the people who turn their guns in are not the people we need to worry about, anyway.

I'm not trying to make a case for assault weapons. As far as I'm concerned, we have gun clubs for people who want to use these weapons. They're called the

Army and the Marine Corps. I don't think civilians should have assault rifles any more than they should have M-60 machine guns.

For home defense, I'd suggest a shotgun. In close quarters and darkness, it would seem the ideal weapon.

On the other hand, if you think the end is near and we'll soon be in a lawless, post-apocalyptic world, then it makes sense to get an assault rifle.

But don't buy one on my say-so. I am not predicting an apocalypse.

JANUARY 19, 2014

'Vigilant' KSDK made a poor choice

Whenever a journalist is accused of an ethical violation, I am there for him. Or her.

Perhaps it's because I have been accused of so many such violations myself, or maybe I just have an old-school view of this business, but the bottom line is I am unashamedly sympathetic to any journalist accused of an ethical lapse. If you are such a journalist and you lose me, you've lost the room.

Bad news for KSDK. They've lost me.

According to a story this newspaper published Friday, KSDK was preparing a story on school safety. A reporter went to Kirkwood High School on Thursday. He walked in unimpeded.

He asked directions to the office. He asked to speak with somebody from security. The secretary said the school resource officer was not in the office. She took the name and phone number of the visitor, who did not identify himself as a reporter. Administrators became alarmed when the visitor asked for the location of a restroom but headed in another direction.

Administrators called the number he had left with the secretary. He did not answer the phone, but the message identified him as a reporter with KSDK. Administrators then called KSDK, but the station refused to confirm or deny the person worked for the station. Even when the administrators said they would have to put the school on lockdown if the visitor's identity remained unknown, the station wouldn't budge.

So the school went on lockdown. That means police were called. Students and teachers huddled fearfully in classrooms.

What was the purpose of letting the school think a gunman might be hiding somewhere in the school? Let's even take it one step further back. Why didn't the reporter just check in with the office, identify himself as a reporter and announce he was doing a story on school security? The station isn't saying. Whatever the reason, the lockdown made a big splash, which, come to think of it, might have been the reason.

If so, it worked. Even I watched KSDK at 10 p.m. Thursday.

Nobody explained the reason for forcing the school to go on lockdown. Instead, we got this sanctimonious statement: "NewsChannel 5 will continue to be vigilant when it comes to the safety of our schools and your children therein."

I wanted to shout at the screen. "We don't want you sneaking around our schools. Just give us news, weather and sports. If you want to scare the bejesus out of kids, scare your own."

Besides, exactly what was the report going to prove? That Kirkwood High School isn't being operated like some kind of prison?

Let me tell you what school had really good security — Sandy Hook Elementary. Doors were locked at 9:30 a.m. Visitors were admitted only after a visual review via a video monitor. Identification was required. KSDK would have approved. But guess what? Adam Lanza shot his way through a glass panel next to the door.

Columbine had a deputy sheriff assigned to the school as a full-time armed school resource officer. That didn't stop Eric Harris and Dylan Klebold. They were students.

The notion that we can make schools — or any place — completely safe is false. Even having armed people around doesn't guarantee anything. One of our worst mass shootings was at an Army base. And, locally, of course, we had the horrific shooting at Kirkwood City Hall. The first two victims were armed police officers.

Kirkwood. That makes this stunt from KSDK even more appalling. Did anybody at that station think about that? Or do they just not care?

These are perilous times. Bad things happen. I suppose a television station can play on our fears. It's probably good for ratings. They can send reporters sneaking around and then point out security lapses. Next week, they'll probably take a gun into the zoo. That could really gin up some fright. "Your children aren't even safe at the zoo!"

That seems to be where society is headed. Certainly, the government does what it can to send us the message: "Be very afraid." After all, if we're afraid, we're more willing to give the government increased authority. We must surrender a little freedom for security. Only a powerful government can protect us. Maybe there is even some truth to that.

But we need a television station to protect us? Really?

"NewsChannel 5 will continue to be vigilant when it comes to the safety of our schools and your children therein."

I think the people at KSDK ought to be very grateful that it is not against the law to be sanctimonious. If it were, they'd be looking at some heavy time.

SEPTEMBER 23, 2011

Whom do Cubs fans here root for now?

There are reputable people in this town who lead secret lives. A prominent downtown lawyer is one of them. He roots for the Cubs.

I called him Thursday morning to see how he felt about the weekend series that starts today.

"This isn't for the paper, is it?" he said, a note of concern in his voice.

"I'm not going to use your name," I said.

You see, this is a tough time for Cubs fans in St. Louis. The entire region is thrilled with the late-season surge that has brought the Cardinals to the brink of the playoffs. And playoff baseball is about more than just sports.

It gives the city national exposure. It means an infusion of money to downtown restaurants, hotels and saloons. In these economic times, the businesses can use the dough. Postseason baseball also brings people together. It makes people feel good, and Lord knows, the people around here can use some feeling good.

But the Cubs stand in the way. They play the Cardinals tonight, Saturday and Sunday. They can step on everybody's dreams.

So you can understand the lawyer's need for anonymity. If he were to admit that he wants to see the Cubs win, he could alienate judges, clients and jurors. How could he win his next trial if he were recognized as the dirty son of a gun who rooted against his fellow St. Louisans?

"How do I feel about the series? It is troubling," he said. "All things considered, I'd like to see the Cubs win two out of three."

"Really?" I asked.

"All right. I'd like to see them sweep," he said. "Let them ruin everything."

I am of the same mind. Almost torn, but not quite. My son is a Cardinals fan and I love him dearly. I want to see him happy. Then, too, there is my own livelihood.

Newspaper sales skyrocket if the Cardinals make the playoffs. If they continue on to the World Series, it's like money in my pocket.

Yet I cannot bring myself to root against the team I grew up with.

My people were Protestants in Northern Ireland - a despised minority. They left Belfast and settled on the south side of Chicago. In the midst of a sea of White Sox fans, they rooted for the Cubs.

So being a Cubs fan in St. Louis does not seem so odd.

St. Louisans are good-hearted people. For the most part, they tend to treat a Cubs fan the way a family treats an alcoholic uncle at the family picnic. They tolerate him. They might even laugh at his jokes. They are affectionate, but they pray that their children don't follow the path that he has chosen. As a Cubs fan, I am accustomed to this attitude that mixes sympathy with condescension.

But this is an unusual time. There is a strange vibe in the air. People are desperate for something good. They are ready to be angry if the Cubs smash their hopes.

Some people might blame this desperation on the tough economy. I suspect it has more to do with the ebb and flow of a baseball team. Cardinals fans have a strong sense of history, and they recognize that this season might mark the end of the La Russa dynasty.

He seems ready to go. Always a solemn man, he seems to be having less fun than ever. You can see him in the dugout, wearing his dark glasses, standing next to Medium Mac, staring joylessly out toward the field.

For most of the year, as the team stumbled and underachieved, the call-in shows and blogs were filled with anti-La Russa comments.

Oh, how he'd like to silence the critics with a championship! That would be the way a Hall of Famer ought to leave. It is hardly a pipe dream. The Cardinals are red hot. If they can just make it into the postseason, they will have more than a decent chance of winning it all.

Next year, then, would be a new start. Minus La Russa, minus Medium Mac, and probably minus Albert Pujols.

So there is a sense of history tied into the current situation. If this is to be the end of an era, let it end well.

But here come the Cubs. As the downtown lawyer said, they could ruin everything.

It makes no sense to root for them this weekend. Why would I root against my own self-interest, and against my family and friends and the city in which I have lived for 31 years?

Because at the core of my being, I am still a small child, lying in bed, listening to Jack Quinlan and Lou Boudreau on my transistor radio. It was thrilling whenever the Cubs won.

It still is.

About the author

Bill McClellan grew up in Chicago and attended the University of Illinois. He flunked out, and was drafted into the Marine Corps.

After the Marines, he attended Arizona State University. He was then hired by the Phoenix Gazette. After his girlfriend was accepted into dental school at Washington University, McClellan moved to St. Louis. He was hired by the Post-Dispatch in 1980 and wrote entertainment listings. He then moved to the City Desk where he worked the night city police beat. He began writing a column in 1983.

He and his wife, Mary, who did indeed become a dentist, have two children, Lorna and Jack. Despite her father's admonitions, Lorna attended the University of Illinois. She graduated with a degree in biology. Jack graduated from the University of Wisconsin with a degree in English.

This is McClellan's fourth collection of columns. He has also written a true-crime book.